INVESTMENT
in the
ENVIRONMENT

INVESTMENT in the ENVIRONMENT

Recent housing, planning and transport policies in Scotland

ERIC GILLETT
Hon. Fellow, Department of Politics,
University of Edinburgh

ABERDEEN UNIVERSITY PRESS

First published 1983
Aberdeen University Press
A member of the Pergamon Group

British Library Cataloguing in Publication Data
Gillett, Eric
Investment in the environment.
1. Regional planning—Scotland
I. Title
361.6′1′09412 HT395.G72

ISBN 0-08-030367-6
ISBN 0-08-030363-3 Pbk

PRINTED IN GREAT BRITAIN
THE UNIVERSITY PRESS
ABERDEEN

CONTENTS

PREFACE

How is public policy formed? What are the influences of different agencies on the process? Is there a theory or a model which can explain all or most of what appears to happen? Is the process democratic, oligarchic or bureaucratic? Is it open or covert?

These questions have been the subject of numberless studies from those of the great political philosophers downwards, and the resulting conclusions have been almost as numerous. This book aims to examine them in the light of events in the past few years in one specific field, that of policy in Scotland towards the man-made environment. Within this field there are many issues of considerable importance to people in Scotland and the quality of the life they lead, such as the state of housing, the decline of council house building and the growth of owner-occupation, including the vexed issue of the right of tenants to buy council houses; the attempts to deal with inner-city decline in Glasgow and elsewhere; the drafting of structure plans and the decisions on hotly-contested planning issues such as the Scotland Gas Project in Fife and the applications for boreholes to conduct research into nuclear waste disposal; the conflict between development and conservation in the countryside; the programme of inter-city road building and the changing attitude to road building within towns and cities; the rivalry between Glasgow, Edinburgh and Prestwick airports; and the special transport problems of the Highlands and Islands. The link between these diverse issues, beyond the fact that they all relate to what should or should not be built and how the resulting environment should be managed, is that they are all the responsibility of the Secretary of State for Scotland, so that an examination of the ways in which decisions on them have been made will illuminate the operation of the system of Scottish government and the possible changes which devolution might have brought or might in future bring about.

This book nevertheless does not claim to be an account of all significant events in the environmental field in Scotland during the period it covers. Since it is concerned with national policy, and the ways in which it is determined, it does not discuss ongoing activities unless there has been a change of policy affecting them. Nor does it deal with the policies and decisions of local authorities and public and private organisations except where they have affected government policy, or government policy has affected them. For these reasons many things of great importance to the Scottish environment do not feature in this book, for example, the water and sewerage service, the cleansing of the rivers, the control of smoke and other pollutants, the fate of buildings of architectural or historic interest, the quality of design of important buildings and the townscape around them, and the many important local authority decisions affecting the environment of the area and the circumstances in which people live. For the most part these matters, important as they are—and sometimes more important in the long run than the matters which have been dealt with here—have been decided within existing national policies, and therefore fall outside the scope of this study of policy-making.

Eric Gillett

Acknowledgements

In writing this book I have received much help from my former colleagues in the Scottish Office by way of suggestions and factual corrections, though I alone am responsible for the choice of topics and the opinions expressed. I should like also to express my gratitude to newer colleagues in the Department of Politics of Edinburgh Unversity, who introduced me into the academic community and gave me guidance on the standards at which I should aim. Many other people have given me interviews and supplied me with material, and to them also I am indebted. Finally I should like to thank my wife for her constant encouragement (and the preparation of the index) and Joyce More for her meticulous care in typing not only the initial text but also the final copy.

Note on Nomenclature

Although most of the topics in this book fall within the ambit of the Scottish Development Department, I mostly use the term 'Scottish Office' in describing (with unavoidable ambiguity) the actions of Scottish Ministers and their officials, reserving the term 'Scottish Development Department' for circulars, memoranda and other published documents bearing the Department's name.

I use the terms 'Conservative' and 'Tory' indiscriminately, changing from one to the other only for the sake of variety.

EG

CHAPTER I

THE BACKGROUND FOR POLICY-MAKING IN SCOTLAND

THE GOVERNMENT MACHINE

On virtually all the matters with which this book deals (and many others besides) the Secretary of State for Scotland has the responsibility for policy-making in Scotland, subject to the Cabinet. His constitutional powers are the same as those of other Cabinet Ministers in their fields - to choose some diverse examples, the Secretary of State for the Environment in English environmental topics, the Secretary of State for Trade in UK trade questions, and the Secretary of State for Foreign and Commonwealth Affairs in external relations. Though these four Ministers have very different subjects to deal with, their constitutional position is the same: subject to the tradition of collective responsibility, to central decisions on resources and finance, and to the agreement of Parliament when it is needed, they each have the power and responsibility to take and enforce decisions on matters which statute, or in some cases the Royal prerogative, delegates to them. All this is obvious to students of British constitutional practice, but it is sometimes not understood that both the strengths and the weaknesses of the Scottish Secretary derive from the same sources as other Cabinet Ministers, and that the degree of administrative and political devolution which exists in Scotland is simply an aspect of Cabinet government. The strength of the arrangement, from the point of view of Scottish interests, is that the Scottish Secretary takes part in the formulation of collective British policy, whether this affects Scotland directly or indirectly, and that other Ministers cannot determine the policy and decisions of the Scottish Office except by collective decision of the Cabinet. This has proved as important under Conservative as under Labour governments, in the former case because the party in power at Westminster must attempt to retain and develop what support it has in Scotland, and in the latter because of the very strength of Labour in Scotland. It is almost unnecessary to say that the danger of losing the influence of the Scottish Secretary in the British Cabinet has been one of the principal reservations which some people have held against devolution. George Younger, in an interview on Radio Scotland in October 1981, declared himself a convert to the view that the present system gives the strongest possible weight to the Scottish voice in government, echoing the view of many of his predecessors.

The corresponding weakness of the system is that the Scottish Office cannot do anything which is contrary to collective Cabinet decisions. (I avoid saying that the Scottish Office can only do what is permitted by the Cabinet, since this would imply a much tighter strait-jacket than in fact exists.) One of the objects of this book will be to examine how far Cabinet decisions (or rather what can be deduced about Cabinet decisions) influence the scope of policy-making in Scotland in the environmental field and how far the views of English departments and their Ministers - in particular the Environment Department and its Secretary of State - influence Scottish policies.

It is important to remember that Cabinet decisions include the vitally important decisions on the allocation of financial resources, because these in so many cases determine the policies which it is practicable to adopt - again a subject of discussion later in this book. It is equally important to remember that they are Cabinet decisions and not the decisions of Treasury Ministers alone: there are plenty of inspired 'leaks' to confirm the belief that Ministers, in spite of their front of collective unanimity, hold very different views on public expenditure, and that Treasury Ministers do not always win. The Scottish Secretary has however since the late '70s operated under a new system, which first grew up as an administrative convenience and was acknowledged in 1979 as a formal policy, under which changes in the Scottish Office expenditure programme, apart from agriculture and industry, are not separately argued, but the total allocated goes down or up by 10/85ths of what is decided in relation to England (and the Welsh Office programme by 5/85ths). As members of the Cabinet, the Scottish and Welsh Secretaries take part in the discussion, and what emerges is a decision on the changes in public expenditure within Great Britain as a whole. The Scottish and Welsh Secretaries are then entitled to allocate their share over programmes within their field of responsibility as they wish. Whether they allocate differently from Ministers for English departments is a matter of operational policy, not determined by the Treasury. We will see some of the effects of this in the environmental field later, but it is a system which George Younger, in giving evidence to the Scottish Select Committee, claimed to give him much more freedom of action. And it is interesting to note that the system applies broadly to those areas where the Scottish Executive would have had discretion under the devolution Bills of the 1970s. The Scottish Secretary is provided by his officials with a factual statement of how much difference a given change in the total expenditure programmes would make, on the 10/85ths basis, to his allocation, and an analysis of various ways in which the total change in his programme might be met. This draws attention to the way in which the changes in expenditure are to be reflected in the programmes in England, as the bigger partner, but discusses the different options open to him in view of existing commitments, previous understandings and Scottish requirements generally. The constraint on him is not the English policy itself,but how far his commitments, his party in Scotland and Scottish public opinion would permit - or demand - differences from the English pattern of expenditure.

Constitutionally, the role of civil servants in this process is the same as in any other sphere of policy - to present the Minister with an analysis of the facts and the possible options as they see them, concluding wherever possible with a positive recommendation. Since both the theory and (in spite of allegations to the contrary) the reality of the matter is that on important questions the decision is that of the Minister himself, it has always been judged important in Britain that the nature of the advice should not be made public, lest the advice, and whether Minister acted upon it, comes to be thought more important than the decision itself. So in the cases discussed in this book the reader must not expect to find what the advice to Ministers was, except in those instances where an official, such as a chief professional adviser or a reporter to a public inquiry, is instructed, by statute or by practice, to make his recommendations known, and even this is not the final advice to the Minister by his senior civil servants.

There is perennial speculation about whether civil servants seek to impose their policies on Ministers and to be obstructive in implementing policies they do not like. Some policies bear the mark of being devised by departments and adopted by Ministers without much enthusiasm, but no Scottish Ministers or ex-Ministers have yet alleged obstruction - unlike one or two prominent English politicians - but in the course of the succeeding case studies we shall see what the evidence shows. The force required to change the momentum of any large body is of course considerable, whether the object is to move it forward or to hold it back, and Government departments are not exempt from this law, particularly in cases where a new departure in policy involves big changes in the administrative structure all the way along the line.

The relationship between Ministers and Parliament will similarly be examined in this book in the light of the specific case studies, distinguishing between the constitutional responsibility of Parliament (for example, to legislate, to vote money, to scrutinise the actions of the executive, and to debate policy in public) and the practical relationship between Ministers and MPs, particularly those of their own party. So long as a Government has a majority, its policies are not much affected by the activities of the Opposition in Parliament, though it must try to maintain superiority in debate. What is of more concern to Ministers in the short term is the attitude of their own back-benchers, which generally has much more importance in policy-making than the views of Opposition parties. Very rarely indeed is a Minister seen to change his policy because of Opposition criticism alone, no matter how numerous the parliamentary questions, the adjournment debates, the 'supply' days, or whatever, and it would not seem that rebutting Opposition points is one of the most difficult of Ministers' tasks. It is support within his own party that a Minister needs, and if a policy founders it is more often than not because of lack of this support.

PARTIES, PRESSURE GROUPS, AND THE MEDIA

This brings us to the question of the functions of the political parties. In one sense, party organisations have no place in the constitutional structure, since their position is not written into legislation or constitutional case-law, but in another sense everything depends on them, since they are the means by which candidates are nominated for election as MPs; leaders and other Ministers must be acceptable to them; and (what is of most importance in this present study) they formulate party policies in the form of manifestos which when an election is won must become Government policy or the party will need to know why.

Manifestos, like other party political decisions, are essentially devised and approved on a UK basis, in the case of the Labour and Conservative parties. The independence of the Scottish end of the parties is strictly limited: they may propose policies, but even if these are limited to Scotland they must be approved by the UK party organisation, since the parties fight elections and aim to gain a majority on a UK basis. Nevertheless the Scottish content of election manifestos in environmental matters is of some interest, as we shall see.

If manifestos represent UK party policy, then so does the government of the majority party represent its UK policy, irrespective of whether it has a majority in Scottish constituencies. Nobody needs reminding that few of the measures applied to Scotland by the government elected in 1979 would have been passed on the votes of Scottish members only. This is not an unprecedented situation, but was given point by contrast with the result which similar voting for a devolved assembly would have had.

The other main agencies with influences over policy-making are the pressure groups and the media. Each is the subject of an extensive literature, and it would be impossible to summarise here the various schools of thought about them. Instead the case studies should show in practice what influences they have had on environmental policy in Scotland. But one or two general points may be made first, with regard to the particular situation in Scotland. The first is that paradoxically both the pressure groups and the media are at the same time more inward-looking than in England and yet strongly affected by English considerations. To take the pressure groups: the majority of those which concern themselves with Scotland as a whole (excluding, that is, locally-oriented groups) are either branches of British organisations, with varying degrees of independence, or have close links with English counterparts and benefit from their greater staffing and research capabilities. But their objectives are firmly related to Scotland, and many of them have a firm expectation of close consultation with the Scottish Office at both Ministerial and official level. Not that this does not take place in England, but in Scotland most well-established associations and interest groups seem to feel that they are better known to the Scottish Office than their English counterparts are to English departments. Most pressure groups concentrate on particular fields of public affairs, having been set up for that purpose, but there are two major bodies which have a much broader concern. The Convention of Scottish Local Authorities, whose consultative functions and influence on policy-making will appear many times in this book, is discussed below. The Scottish Trades Union Congress is a pressure group of a unique kind. Not a policy-making body, even within the trade union world, it is very active in considering questions in almost every field of public affairs, passing resolutions, and making its views known to governments, but its resolutions sometimes have an unreality which makes them an embarrassment to Labour governments, and the object of amusement to Tories. It is traditional, however, that Ministers should agree to meet representatives of the STUC if requested, and Labour Ministers particularly have a close and time-consuming relationship with them. It is difficult to say that they have any influence on environmental matters, even under a Labour government.

Turning to the Press, most of the mass-circulation dailies, where they carry serious news, features, and leading articles, give much more attention to employment, inflation, police, and public order questions than to environmental affairs. Even housing topics, unless they contain an element of scandal, generally merit only a small paragraph on an inner page. Just occasionally a tabloid paper will select an environmental topic, such as test boring for nuclear waste research, for a campaign, and the effect of this can be considerable if it prompts people to write to their MPs, particularly government back-benchers. The 'quality' papers' coverage of Scottish news is of course much more wide-ranging and complete, and they provide much of the basic information about Scottish public affairs needed by people in positions of influence. Serious discussion of Scottish problems could hardly go on without them, because of the sketchy coverage by the tabloids and the ephemeral nature of television and radio news. Feature articles in those papers, whether by staff writers or invited contributors, are an important factor in public debate: they can be one-sided, as speeches in Parliament can be one-sided, but they maintain to a considerable extent the distinction between fact and comment and the best of them are well researched and provide useful summaries of the history of the subject at issue. Leading articles command less attention, written as they are in haste and without much opportunity for consideration in depth. Leading articles on national environmental policy are infrequent, though less so on local affairs in the home city of the newspaper concerned. Both feature articles, and to a lesser extent leaders, make a direct contribution to policy by leading to questions being put to and points taken up with MPs and Scottish Ministers. On the whole newspapers of all kinds tend to be rather less partisan about environmental matters than about political, economic and industrial affairs. Nor do they often give front-page treatment to them. Radio and television coverage of environmental policy matters is largely direct reporting: it would be difficult to find evidence of consistent bias such as the Glasgow Media Group claim over industrial issues and labour relations. Sometimes, however, the fact that Ministers are generally in London while pressure groups are in Scotland means that the latter get better TV coverage, or make a better showing because they are not face to face with the Minister concerned. Major TV and radio features on Scottish environmental affairs are rather uncommon; one of the few exceptions is discussed in the chapter on inner city problems.

In environmental affairs, local authorities, who are the main executives, might be expected to play a major part in policy-making. One of the main objects in forming a single association, the Convention of Scottish Local Authorities, after the reorganisation of local government, was to improve the ability to negotiate with central government; and COSLA, its committees, and its staff play a busy role in considering government proposals and commenting on them in detail, as well as briefing and lobbying MPs. But on the evidence of the case studies COSLA appears to accept, in Scottish political debate, a reactive rather than an initiating role; it responds to Government proposals rather than takes the initiative itself. Perhaps it is not the function of local authorities in a parliamentary democracy to try to shape national policy and perhaps impossible for them to do so on subjects which are a matter of party strife, since they are unlikely to be able to speak with one voice themselves - one only has to instance the subject of the sale of council houses to see how impossible it would be for COSLA, representing councils of such differing views to take a united initiative. Against this, it is possible for COSLA to agree on opposition to cuts in rates support grant, though even here with different degrees of emphasis. So in the main its role is to reply to government consultation, and on many subjects it has a statutory right to be consulted. Having consulted, governments take account of practical criticisms and detailed suggestions for improvement of proposals, but ignore comments on matters where there is fundamental political disagreement. The strength of local authorities lies not so much in their ability to resist or modify government decisions, as in the administrative discretion they enjoy in many aspects of their work.

Rather as the organisations of local government react to rather than initiate new Scottish policies, so do the professions, important as they are in other aspects of public life, abstain from seeking a major role in environmental policy-making. The legal profession has an important role in interpreting the law and in commenting on the legal practicability of new proposals. Architects and planners see their main role as designers of buildings and of the environment rather than as policy makers. The professions connected with finance and industry have little direct concern with environmental policy, though of course they try to influence public expenditure policy, which in turn determines the amount of resources devoted to housing and other environmental subjects. Academics contribute to policy-making, in the main, indirectly, through the books they write and through the research commissions which they undertake. It is probably through membership of political parties and pressure groups, rather than through their professional organisations, that professional people exert most influence over decisions in this field.

This chapter has attempted to give no more than a brief preliminary outline of the main agencies involved in policy-formation and to indicate the type of power and influence they might be expected to exercise. Before looking at particular aspects of recent environmental policy in Scotland to discern, as far as possible, how decisions were made and who contributed to making them, it is necessary to consider the relation of environmental issues to the central policy issue which has bulked so large in Scottish political debate and public discussion in the late 1970s and since, namely devolution.

THE DEVOLUTION PROPOSALS OF THE 1970s

In one sense there is little to say about devolution and environmental policy, since there was never any serious doubt that the Secretary of State's main environmental functions, and his control over local authorities and appointed bodies exercising them locally, would be devolved to the Scottish assembly and executive if devolution took place. Housing, planning, roads, ferries, buses and other local transport, and the other subjects with which we are concerned had always, or for a number of years, been Secretary of State responsibilities, and the principle on which the Labour devolution proposals were based (with no dissent from other supporters of devolution) was that these responsibilities should be devolved unless they impinged on matters such as taxation and the economy, which the Labour government regarded as UK matters. The intense debate on the extent of devolution hardly affected environmental policy. If there was to be devolution, nearly all environmental policy would be handed over to the new Scottish institutions; in the meantime the Secretary of State would carry on as before, while avoiding as far as possible decisions on matters which could and should be left to them. Thus the Scotland Bill 1977, like the Scotland and Wales

Bill in the previous session, proposed to give the assembly power to legislate on housing, rent regulation, town and country planning, building control, derelict land, control of pollution, countryside conservation and development for public enjoyment, passenger transport subsidies, roads, ferries and aerodromes, water supplies, ancient monuments and historic buildings. Within those fields, however, some specific matters were reserved to Parliament and the UK administration - mainly things which might impinge on the activities of UK Ministers exercising their functions in Scotland, and some matters thought to be best regulated on a UK basis, such as control of pollution by vehicles, and regulation of building societies.

The devolved services were to be financed by block grant from the UK government, not by separate taxation. Whether the Scottish assembly and executive should have powers of taxation to finance their responsibilities was of course and has continued to be one of the main elements if not the preponderating element in devolution debates. The debate was on the question of taxation powers in general, however, rather than on the financing of environmental, health, education, or other functions in particular. Matters might have been different if it had been known just how bitter the disagreement on public expenditure after the 1979 elections was to be, and how much a Conservative government at Westminster would be likely to have cut the block vote for the Scottish assembly and limited its freedom of action. As it was, the supporters of Labour-type devolution claimed that the assembly would receive a not insufficient block grant, and the expectation was that it would be based on recent patterns of expenditure. The Labour government's line was that the grant could not be based on a formula, but must be a political decision.[1] Nevertheless a study was instituted to collect objective information on needs and standards of public service in all four countries of the UK, to help in making an informed judgment. This was completed early in 1979, but not published until several months after the repeal of the devolution acts.[2]

---

(1) 'Our changing democracy' Cmnd 6348, 1975

(2) Needs Assessment Study Report HMSO December 1979

THE BACKGROUND FOR POLICY-MAKING

So far as environmental services were concerned (housing, roads, public transport and water), it indicated that the expenditure needed per head of population to maintain the same standards in Scotland as in England was close to the expenditure which had actually been allocated in recent years. In other words, past allocations had been about right as far as an objective study of needs could demonstrate. But even if this pattern of allocations had been reflected in the calculation of the block grant after devolution, it would not have protected the environmental services in Scotland from the effect of a policy of cutting public expenditure as a whole adopted by the government in Westminster.

One significant omission from the environmental powers given to the Scottish assembly was legislation on taxing land values. This exclusion, presumably dictated by the Labour government's decision not to give the assembly any powers of taxation, would have prevented it taking any new and distinctively Scottish approach to the problem of betterment - the increase in the value of land arising from the grant of planning permission. At the Great Britain level, three Labour administrations since the Second World War had created legislative and organisational arrangements to recover some of these increased values for the community at large - the Central Land Board in the late 1940s, the Land Commission in the 1970s, and the Community Land Scheme in the 1970s. None had been a great success; the first two had been abolished by succeeding Conservative governments, and the third was to be similarly dealt with, but a Scottish assembly might have wished to have another try. However, the Labour government was not prepared to give it that freedom. It would be wrong to lay too much stress on the denial of these powers to the assembly, since in Scottish attitudes to planning there was not present to the same extent as in housing policy a tradition of legislating in a substantially different way from England and Wales, and it is unlikely that a Scottish assembly would have wanted to tax land values if they were not similarly taxed in England and Wales, because of the fear that it would have made industrialists and other developers favour sites south of the Border.

This is one example of the dilemma which would have been faced by the assembly in all fields, even where the devolution Bills would have given it power to act.

INVESTMENT IN THE ENVIRONMENT

To take others, the assembly could have empowered local authorities to take over landlords' houses; it could have slashed the road programme so as to double the ferry subsidies to the islands or abolish tolls on the Forth and other road bridges; it could have taken a very tough line with industries responsible for pollution. But measures such as these could in some degree have made investment and development in Scotland less attractive than in England, and this would inevitably have been a significant consideration in deciding whether to adopt radically different policies from those in England. And this dilemma will face any future assembly, whatever the extent of its nominal powers.

In a later chapter I speculate as to what might have been the course of events in the environmental field if devolution had been adopted. For the moment it is only necessary to say that despite some underlying problems, there was no dissent from the proposition that if devolution took place the assembly and executive would have nearly all the powers over housing, planning, transport, and other environmental matters which had previously been exercised from the Scottish Office. Since the referendum and the repeal of the Scotland Act that attitude has persisted. The issue of devolution will not be determined by opinions on responsibility for environmental questions.

CHAPTER II

SCOTTISH HOUSING POLICIES

Many arguments have been conducted over the question whether housing is a social or an economic subject (few would classify it as primarily an environmental topic, although there is a strong contention that the environmental failings of housing strategy are responsible for some of its most intractable problems). The arguments are not just a matter of terminology; how you classify housing tends to reflect or determine your views on housing policy objectives. Those who regard housing as a social subject tend to favour objectives such as redistribution of wealth, the reduction of disparities in living standards, and the amelioration of social conditions, while those who regard housing as mainly an economic question tend to think that housing strategies should be determined by what people are prepared to pay for in the same way as other necessities such as food and clothing.

Naturally there is a spectrum of opinion between those two extremes, but in broad terms they mirror the views of the Labour and Conservative supporters. Thus, for example, the Transport and General Workers Union said in August 1977 that "it is wasteful, immoral, and ultimately damaging to treat housing as a commodity instead of as an elementary social provision". Even in periods of Conservative government the social objectives have tended to prevail, perhaps because the Conservative party committed itself for 20 years or more to beating Labour on the question of the number of houses built in the public sector. This enabled local authorities, mainly Labour, to pursue the objective of house building irrespective of costs and rents. Anyway, housing in Scotland for thirty years after the Second World War was in practice handled much like services such as education, with the public sector overwhelmingly predominant not only in the resources devoted to it but also in the amount and nature of public discussion. Even the attempt of the Conservative administration of 1970-74 to reduce subsidies and increase rents did not greatly alter the picture.

LABOUR'S 'GREEN PAPER' 1977

It is all the more surprising that a 'wide-ranging examination of housing policies and finance' should have been undertaken, in Scotland as well as in England and Wales, by the Labour government elected in 1974, which resulted in a document which may in future years be seen as contributing more towards changed housing policies than more spectacular changes such as tenants' rights to buy council houses. "Scottish Housing: A Consultative Document" of June 1977 (the Housing Green Paper) is therefore taken as the starting point for this discussion of recent and current housing policies.

This review was described as being 'carried out within the Scottish Development Department with the advice of a sub-committee of the Scottish Housing Advisory Committee'. Thus from the start, the Government department concerned was more implicated in the work than it would have been in a report of SHAC itself or one of its sub-committees. Since it was a consultative document, Bruce Millan and his Ministerial team were not formally committed to it, and described it as outlining "policy options which we would want to be widely discussed before we take firm decisions". They did not dissociate themselves, however, from the factual analysis of the housing situation which in many respects is the most significant part of the Green Paper.

There is little evidence that the Government, either in Scotland or in England and Wales, were being pressed to review policy in any fundamental way by public opinion, pressure groups, the Press and television (which at that time were concentrating on the question of homelessness), MPs or, least of all, their own party. It started and finished as a departmental review, scrutinised and revised in detail by Ministers, but characteristically the product of the government machine rather than of outside pressure. It was undertaken "in parallel with a review covering England and Wales", and acknowledged that it reached the same conclusions on "those aspects of housing finance - such as mortgage finance - which for reasons of taxation and practical administration have to be looked at together". Furthermore, its suggestions on future policy were very similar. But proposals which would not seem very surprising in England looked quite revolutionary against the background of traditional policies in Scotland - in particular, the encouragement given to owner-occupation, the proposals to permit the sale of council houses in accordance with local housing plans (which were themselves a concept which had been put into effect earlier than in England and Wales), and the criticism of the rigidity of councils' house-letting policies.

The section of the Green Paper which foreshadowed the most fundamental change in successive governments' approach to housing was perhaps that which analysed future needs. Having shown that the standard of housing was now higher than in England and Wales (a challenge to traditional beliefs) it concluded that even on the highest estimates the need for public sector building was little more than half the level of the previous ten years, and on the lowest estimates of average household size and vacancy rate "the need appears very small indeed". This was emphasised by pointing out that if council house building continued at 25,000 per year the result would be a high vacancy rate, under-occupation, large-scale demolition, or a combination of these.

From this the Green Paper proceeded to an analysis of the objectives of future policy and the means of achieving them which represented a considerable departure from earlier Labour policy. Thus government subsidies would not be calculated by formulae enshrined in statute but calculated by the Scottish Office on an estimate of "the aggregate expenditure which authorities will need to incur" and of what "they can reasonably be expected to obtain from rents and rates"; rents in the long run would have to "stand in a reasonable relationship to costs"; the housing system needed adjustment to cater for people who need houses quickly or for short periods or for employment reasons; it should be easier for people to become home owners; some public rented houses might be sold in response to the demand; there was no case for altering tax relief on mortgage interest; there should be better management of council houses; house-letting rules should be published; and the Government would work out "how to apply the principle of security of tenure to the public sector".

It was quickly realised that these proposals, coming from a Labour government, were very radical. "The Scotsman" said that the Green Paper could easily be mistaken for the product of a Tory administration, and it was indeed generally welcomed by the Tories during a Debate in the Scottish Grand Committee in July 1977, while Labour MPs were much more restrained. The Scottish National Party's response was to call for a national housing finance corporation, cheaper loans for local authorities, and index-linked rebates. SHELTER said that the proposals of the Green Paper could lead to "a stigmatisation of the public sector" which could be disastrous. The STUC executive drafted a memorandum generally favourable to the Green Paper, but Congress itself passed a resolution calling for 50,000 new houses a year, which Bruce Millan had to sidestep when he attended its next conference. Then in March 1978 the Scottish Conference of the Labour Party condemned the Green Paper in its entirety, demanding instead all the traditional Labour grass-roots remedies - restoration of all housing subsidies, more public ownership, and the transfer to housing authorities of the money being given to private landlords.

Nevertheless Bruce Millan and Hugh Brown continued to defend and implement the Green Paper. Thus Hugh Brown was saying in October 1977 that the Green Paper "dispelled a few myths. Now we need a new approach if we are to succeed in tackling the residual older problems and the wider-ranging and awkward new problems". Legislation was introduced to replace the multifarious subsidies by a single (and Government-controlled) housing support grant, and back-bench resistance was inneffective. A clause removing the old £39 per year limit on council rent increases was successfully incorporated. The new Housing (Financial Provisions)(Scotland) Bill also included provisions welcome on all sides, such as repairs grants for needy owner-occupiers, and increased Government grant on local rent rebates. Local authorities were asked to draw up comprehensive housing plans for their areas and encouraged to include in them schemes for the controlled selling of council houses. Hugh Brown also said that they would have to be pressured into making land available for owner-occupation in inner cities, even at a loss. The Scottish Housing Advisory Committee was instructed to report on council house-letting policy. Scottish Ministers stopped short at first of English Ministers' proposals at the end of 1978 to give security of tenure to council tenants, and proposed instead a tenants' charter which amounted to a code of practice without statutory force, but had given way on this by February 1979. It was not necessary for Scottish Ministers to take any steps to restrict the number of council houses being built in accordance with the analysis in the Green Paper, because local authorities were doing this of their own volition, and the Government were able to say that they had not cut the amount of capital investment in housing to less than local authorities' demands, and had allowed for a modest increase in real terms. In fact the increases planned for two and three years ahead were of the order of 15%, to help to offset the dramatic fall in starts on new council houses, which fell from over 12,000 in 1975 to less than 5,000 in 1979.

With the defeat, in UK terms, of the Labour party in the 1979 election the Green Paper ceased to have any formal position in Government thinking. Nevertheless, as will be shown, large parts of it were adopted by the Conservative administration, and its analysis of reduced housing needs helped to justify the Tories' policy on capital investment authorisations to housing authorities. If political opinions on housing had not become polarised by the single issue of the sale of council houses, the Green Paper of 1977 might well have formed the basis of a tacitly agreed housing policy, and even if that is now unattainable the Green Paper's factual analysis of need is likely to remain the basis of official advice to Ministers on housing for some years to come.

THE RIGHT TO BUY

For the whole of the post-war period, housing policy had been governed by the urgent necessity to remedy the deficiencies in the housing stock. However, under the Conservatives the question of need became subsidiary to the question of tenants' rights to buy the houses they lived in. This has predominated in Conservative thinking to a remarkable extent, and during the 1970s the party moved from encouraging local authorities to sell to giving tenants the absolute right to buy at very considerable discounts. The qualifications which originally accompanied the right to buy disappeared; thus the Tory manifesto for Scotland of February 1974 promised the right to buy "on reasonable terms", and also subject to appeal by local authorities on specified grounds, but the October manifesto dropped the right of appeal and promised one-third discounts. In May 1977 Teddy Taylor said that the sale of council houses would be conducted "at a controlled pace"; but the 1979 manifesto promised legislation in the first session to give the right to buy at discounts up to one-half, with safeguards only for rural areas and sheltered housing for the elderly.

What was the origin of this policy? In the earlier forms of simply allowing local authorities to sell, it was not particularly contentious in England, and even in Scotland Labour Ministers were prepared to grant requests from local authorities for permission to sell if this did not endanger the waiting list. Early in 1977, Hugh Brown was saying that he was not against selling in the right circumstances, but that this was no panacea. Somewhat later Labour Ministers were willing to advocate greater house ownership, and set up the Scottish Home Ownership Forum to discuss how it should be achieved. Bruce Millan however reacted angrily when some members of that body advocated private ownership on a scale which could clearly only be reached by massive council house sales. So for Labour Ministers private ownership was never the main consideration, and for many of their supporters it was downright bad. The unqualified right of tenants to buy council houses is a very different matter, stemming from the Tory belief in the innate value of ownership above all other considerations. The Tory commitment to the right to buy originated as a party doctrine, and enthusiastic advocacy of it is still largely confined to Conservative politicians. That it did not stem from a Green Paper or the representations of pressure groups is no criticism: it is the function of political parties to formulate ideas based on their own view of society and the needs of the country: they do not have to depend on external pressures or social surveys. And the Tory policy in Scotland hardened towards an unrestricted right to buy in response to the refusal of many Labour-administered councils to sell at all.

SCOTTISH HOUSING POLICIES

To bring the policy into effect required legislation, but this presented no problems precisely because it was party dogma, and the Conservatives had a secure majority at Westminster. Unlike some political objectives, it was one which could be achieved by a relatively straightforward change in the law; you cannot, for example, solve the problem of the inner cities by legislation, but you can confer a statutory right to buy. Furthermore, giving the right to buy cost nothing and was therefore not constrained by public expenditure policies. (The question whether public funds would gain or lose in the long run was more arguable; a document[1] issued by the Government during the passage of the Bill seemed to indicate that it all depended on what assumptions you worked.) And the policy has the advantage of being irreversible once sales have taken place; a future Government could only legislate to stop further sales, and the danger of this would tend to encourage, rather than deter, purchases while the right exists. (The Labour Party did indeed commit themselves at the end of 1981 to abolish the right to buy, but promised that they would not act vindictively or spitefully towards those who had already bought.)

The Bills giving the right to buy were among the major Parliamentary events of the 1979-80 session, as regards both Scotland and England; and with a secure majority and a firm conviction Tory Ministers took pride in putting them through. High claims were made for the policy: Michael Heseltine said that no single act of social policy was more likely to change attitudes and opportunities than the enfranchisement of council tenants, and he and his Scottish colleagues consistently refused to accept the argument that they were cutting down the number of houses available to people in need, which was the root of opposition to the proposals, argued at length up and down the country, inside and outside Parliament. Established positions were maintained; few people were heard to say that there was truth on both sides, for example, that the sale of a council house to a sitting tenant does not immediately reduce the number of houses available to the council for allocation, but in the long run it will do so, as the purchasers leave or die and their houses are sold instead of being

---

[1] Appraisal of the Financial Effect of Council House Sales, DOE, January 1980

relet. A further claim by the Opposition was that sales would tend to be concentrated in the better housing schemes, and the average quality of the stock in council hands would decline, and there was much assertion and counter-assertion about this, without either side having, as yet, any statistics to prove its case.

With the Conservative party united on the question, there was no need or scope for major policy initiatives on the part of the Scottish Ministerial team. The Scottish Bill when published however did show some differences from the English Bill, apart from those necessitated by the differences in the basic law in both countries. One which was to provoke much argument was the absence of any special restriction on the right to buy in rural areas: English Ministers, conscious of the demand for holiday and retirement homes in parts of rural England, included in the Housing Bill a provision that without the permission of the local authority houses in national parks and areas of outstanding natural beauty could only be resold by their tenant-purchasers to people who already lived or worked in the area. Scottish Ministers rejected the case for restrictions, arguing that the demand for second homes was less in rural Scotland (and, they might have added, the quality and style of most council housing in country areas was not likely to make it very attractive to buyers) and that in these circumstances council tenants in the country should not be deprived of the unfettered right to buy which was available in the towns. This was to prove one of the few points on which they had to make a concession, and that was to satisfy their own supporters, not to give way to the Opposition. Where more than a third of the council houses in a rural area had been sold, the local authority, with central government sanction, was empowered to demand the first option to repurchase houses subsequently sold.

A difference from the English Bill which proved to be very useful in practice was a provision which allowed a tenant to apply to the Lands Tribunal to take over his application to buy and secure a title for him in case of dilatoriness or procrastination by the council. This proved easier to operate than the English provisions under which the Secretary of State for the Environment's officials had to take over the processing of applications to buy.

SCOTTISH HOUSING POLICIES

Less controversial Bills than the Tenants' Rights Bill are often modified and improved by a process of consultation with interested pressure groups, professional organisations, and the Convention of Scottish Local Authorities. In this case there was clearly no scope for compromise on matters of principle, and although consultations were opened with COSLA the Scottish Office emphasised that they would only relate to minor practical improvements. Pressure groups such as Shelter were implacably opposed to the unrestricted right to buy, and concentrated on getting MPs to move amendments which would exclude or limit the right to buy houses in rural areas, and houses of a kind normally let to the elderly. The Scottish Branch of the Institute of Housing was typical of many in proposing that local authorities should have power to limit sales so as to leave enough houses, and houses of the right type, to meet their statutory obligations. Like the STUC, it was concerned that there would be no protection against local authorities being forced to sell in an unbalanced way.

In spite of opposition, the Government pressed on. Constitutionally and politically they were well placed to do so, as no government is under any obligation to give way to pressure groups any more than to the Parliamentary opposition. A few concessions were made on other aspects of tenants' rights, but the right to buy stood intact. Not until the day before the Parliamentary summer recess of 1980, when the House of Lords passed four amendments to the English Bill against Government advice, was there a hitch. The need to return the Bill to the Commons endangered the chance of making it law before the summer break, which the Tories were desperately anxious to secure, so that tenants could start the process of buying houses from unwilling councils. As the price for getting the Bill, the Government accepted a restriction, in both England and Scotland, on the sale of houses for the elderly. To satisfy their own supporters, moreover, Scottish Ministers had to come some way to the English position on the sale of houses in rural areas, by giving assurances that action could be taken if too many houses were being bought as holiday or second homes for town dwellers. Though the Opposition could thus exploit the Parliamentary situation and the disquiet within the Tory party to force a concession on relatively marginal issues, they could not prevent the granting of the right of tenants in general to buy, and since they probably did not want to be held responsible for delaying security of tenure and other aspects of tenants' rights they did not try to place any other procedural obstacle in the way of both the English and the Scottish Bills becoming law.

Subsequent events in the rearguard campaign of a few recalcitrant local authorities belong to the realm of administration rather than policy-making, but form an interesting study in the relations between and the relative power of central and local government. Although the majority of councils were opposed to having to sell their houses to tenants, nearly all of them began to process applications. Dundee, having been reported in August 1980 as intending to go as far as they could to frustrate the Act, simply let the applications lie. As a result George Younger decided to use the very powerful machinery available under the Local Government (Scotland) Act 1973 to declare a council in default, and if necessary to obtain a court order for the performance of whatever it was that the council had failed to do. A public inquiry in February 1981 found Dundee to be in default, and the Secretary of State directed a timetable for dealing with applications to buy. There was no sign of further resistance. In the case of Stirling, the report of the public inquiry in May and June 1981 established that the council were returning to applicants, without comment, any application forms with an error in them, however small, and had decided to survey only one house per week, which made it impossible to make offers to sell within 3 months, as the Act requires. They had also decided to ask applicants for a £25 deposit; the inquiry reporter found this reasonable but not authorised by the Act. He thought that the main reason for the council's non-compliance with the Act was the failure of officials to give adequate advice, but the outsider may speculate that the council were not over-anxious to get advice, particularly since, in the words of the reporter, the council "do not appear at any time to have considered the time limits seriously". In this case too the default powers appear to have persuaded the council to toe the statutory line.

As well as the general default power available to the Secretary of State, effective use was also made, in the course of 1981, of the provisions enabling tenants to take delayed applications to the Lands Tribunal. 800 cases had been referred to the Tribunal by November 1981, and extra staff were taken on to deal with those cases, which frequently arose from councils trying to impose conditions on sales which were unacceptable to the tenants. Given the comprehensiveness of the procedures available against local authorities, and the unwillingness of councillors to break the law on this issue or to become martyrs like the Clay Cross councillors of the early 1970s, the means available to resist Government policy as translated into statute were few. Conveyancing problems caused delays for a time: Scottish Special Housing Association houses on a number of sites in Glasgow were built on land still owned by the council, and until the SSHA had a title to the land they could not transfer that title to any of their tenants who wanted to buy, and consequently could not sell. The District Council claimed that there was nothing in the Tenants' Rights Act to force them to sell land, and that they were not deliberately frustrating the Act, any more than they were by other administrative problems for which they were criticised by the Government. Using both the carrot and stick technique, Scottish Ministers announced in November 1981 that an Order would be made transferring land to the SSHA, and reached an understanding with the council that if they improved the rate at which sales of their own houses were completed an additional capital allocation of £4 million would be made available.

What has all this achieved in the way of diversifying ownership of the housing stock in Scotland? Scottish Ministers were very satisfied with the sale of 14,000 council houses in 1981-82 against an estimate of 5,000, and presumably this means a lot of purchasers satisfied by the chance of buying their homes at a very substantial discount. Even if all the 56,000 applications to buy which had been made by March 1982 resulted in sales, this amounts however to little over 5% of public sector houses, and on the assumption that there was a pent-up demand to buy (and an eagerness to buy now in case a Labour government came to power and abolished the right to buy) it seems unlikely that the rate can be maintained. In the end, the policy of the right to buy will probably not justify either the excessive fears or the wider expectations which it has aroused. What is now needed as a basis of a rational future policy is research into the satisfactions of purchasers, in money terms and otherwise, the types of houses which are being sold, the effect on the stock available for letting, and the financial consequences to councils. But perhaps it is too much to hope that policy in an area such as this will ever be based on objective study.

THE HOUSING CUTS

Although the right-to-buy issue occupied so much time and energy from 1979 onwards, it was not the only aspect of Conservative housing policy in Scotland. The other most significant policy was that of cutting the amount of resources allocated towards public sector housing. There were steep reductions in spending under Labour, but broadly speaking this simply reflected decreased demand for resources by local authorities. The Tories, however, regarded housing cuts below the level of local authority demand as one of the main ways of reducing public expenditure, given the fact that earlier promises to beat Labour at house-building had been dropped from the manifestos of the 1970s, and that the overall condition of the housing stock had been confirmed by the Labour Green Paper as rather better in Scotland than in England. It is also fair to say that in housing, unlike most other fields of high public expenditure, there is a large and growing private sector alternative, and the argument over cutting the public sector is not about the total housing requirement but about the extent to which the public sector must meet needs which are not met by private building for owner-occupation. This is certainly a wide field for argument, but at least there is room for maintaining that public sector housing is primarily needed only to provide the types of housing which the private sector cannot, while cuts in fields such as the roads programme and education mean fewer new roads and schools, because there is no practicable alternative in the private sector. The formal statement of Tory policy is given in the Public Expenditure White Paper of March 1980, which said that "The Government have had regard to the present size and condition of the housing stock, trends in household formation and the capacity of the private sector to meet housing needs". This might have been said by a Labour government, pursuing "Green Paper" lines of thought, but the conclusions drawn by the Tories were very different. As can be seen from the table of actual and planned public expenditure on housing in Scotland the Labour administration, in

ACTUAL AND PLANNED PUBLIC EXPENDITURE ON HOUSING IN SCOTLAND (£ MILLION)

White Paper on Public Expenditure	Date	Price basis	Year 1975-76	1976-77	1977-78	1978-79	1979-80	1980-81	1981-82	1982-83	1983-84	1984
Cmnd.7049	Jan.78	1977 survey	624	607	581	579	617	640	652			
" 7439	Jan.79	1978 survey	658	636	605	607	638	659	681	690		
" 7841	Mar.80	1979 survey	742	710	671	652	702	603	520	470	410	
" 8175	Mar.81	1980 survey	861	819	770	745	765	687	614	540	460	
" 8494	Mar.82	Cash		538	535	575	739	783	755	739	650	650
" 8789	Feb.83	Cash			536	580	729	780	707	713	656	650

NOTES:

1. Figures to the left of the line are historical: figures to the right are future proposals.

2. The adoption of the cash basis in 1982 makes direct comparison with the White Papers for earlier years impossible, without the application of the price conversion percentages given in section 5.12 of Cmnd.8494.

3. The February 1983 White Paper assumes 5% inflation between 1982-83 and 1983-84. This must be taken into account in considering the likely value, in purchasing power, of the expenditure for the two years.

their public expenditure White Papers of January 1978 and January 1979, were planning to restore housing expenditure in 'real' or 'volume' terms to the levels of the mid-1970s and more within three or four years. These plans would not have to be implemented until after an election, but in any case, a year later the Conservative Government were planning to reduce expenditure in the same period by 40%. In the first year they aimed to reduce expenditure by 14%, and the March 1981 White Paper shows that they actually achieved a 10% reduction. In March 1982 their plan was to reduce expenditure in cash terms from £755m in 1981/82 to £739m in 1982/83. In 'real' or 'volume' terms this meant a planned reduction of about 11%, with a further reduction of about 20% in 1983/84, or more if inflation was higher than was allowed for. The government's wish was that all those reductions would be made on current expenditure, that is to say by cutting government and local authorities' subsidies to the housing accounts and increasing rents correspondingly, and funds were made available to maintain the level of house improvement and council building. George Younger and his colleagues could thus say that if house improvement and council building fell below the levels envisaged in their Labour predecessors' Green Paper it was not their fault.

The selection of housing as one of the major areas for cuts in current expenditure is pre-eminently a policy worked out in the Conservative party itself, with virtually no contribution from other agencies. Conservative leaders and MPs have for years criticised public subsidies to keep rents down, and they saw, in the public sector housing programme, one of the easiest ways to cut or contain public expenditure as a whole, and one which in their view was fully justified by the low percentage of their income (about 5% of average manual male earnings) which public sector tenants had to spend on rent. Outside the Conservative party, there were many interests and pressure groups which wanted a reduction in public expenditure, but they rarely singled out housing. Nearly all Press and TV comment, both locally and nationally, was and continues to be about the defects in housing - the shortage of houses for the homeless, the elderly, and the disabled, the deterioration of older houses, the problem of dampness, and the appalling condition of many council estates. Even in the House of Commons

SCOTTISH HOUSING POLICIES

Tory MPs found it easier to draw attention to the steep decline in council house building under Labour than to advocate increasing rents. But even though the choice of housing subsidies for cuts was a party decision, with little overt encouragement from elsewhere, the Conservatives, with a secure majority and a party united on reducing public expenditure, were well placed to enforce their policy by the exercise of executive powers, namely the control of capital expenditure through the capital authorisations procedure and of current expenditure through Housing Support Grant. The former is an extremely powerful weapon: originally devised to stop unwise and un-credit-worthy borrowing, it has become a major tool for determining local authority expenditure in regard to capital and so dictating or at least circumscribing their building programmes, without attracting more than a fraction of the publicity given to attempts to keep increases in rates down. In housing, as will be shown below, it was the means adopted by George Younger for penalising local authorities (or rather their building programmes) who were not prepared to follow his policy on current housing expenditure, namely keeping down subsidies from the rates. This apart, his policy on the size of the local authority housing investment programme was not as severe as was claimed. It is true that by 1980-81, the gross capital expenditure had fallen to £251 million, following a trend established long before the Tories came into office, but George Younger was prepared to authorise an increase to £277 million the following year,provided local authorities met his current expenditure requirements[1], and a similar proposal of a real increase in the volume of building and improvement under council auspices was on offer in 1982. Within these figures, expenditure on council mortgages and improvement grants to owner-occupiers was given special priority - this was possible because the Labour Government, in abandoning detailed controls over how local authorities spent their capital, had retained the practice of separate capital allocations for council house building and improvement on the one hand, and assistance to owner-occupiers on the other. This neatly matched the Conservatives' policy of giving preference to the latter; they were able to allocate resources to local authorities for mortgages and improvement grants without their being

[1] Minutes of evidence to Committee on Scottish Affairs, 15 June 1981 and 16 June 1982

diverted to the council house accounts. In 1982 the government not only increased the rate of grant to householders for improvement to 90%, but removed any limit on expenditure for this purpose by local authorities for the remainder of 1982/83. The programme for council houses was nevertheless boosted by the Government's decision to credit to it the proceeds of the sale of council houses, to the tune of over £40 million for the year 1982/83. In January 1982 the Government announced that all receipts from house sales in any area would be added to the capital allocations for council house building and improvement. The capital allocation system was thus being used to encourage local authorities to promote sales as it had already been used for two years to encourage rent increases.

One aspect of the policy on housing cuts which is of special interest is the extent to which housing associations have been exempted. Although so well financed by public money (enjoying in fact a uniquely advantageous form of deficit financing) they did not forfeit Conservative favour, and both the 1974 and 1979 manifestos promised special aid to the housing association movement "which has an important role in bridging the gap between owner-occupation and renting from the public sector" and "could help to meet special needs, including those of the elderly and the disabled, the young family which does not wish to settle permanently in a particular area and perhaps the young single person moving to a new job". With the exception of housing for the elderly and disabled, to which a number of housing associations have given particular attention, this was more a hope than a statement of fact, because so much of the work of housing associations is in rehabilitating existing property and returning it to existing tenants. But added to the special efforts made by the Scottish Federation of Housing Associations to show the new Ministers the work they were doing, it was enough to ensure that the Conservative administration kept the housing associations comfortably afloat. Between 1979-80 and 1980-81, when local authority capital expenditure went down from £303 million to £251 million, allocations to housing associations went up from £45 million to £54 million, and an even greater increase was acceptable to the government for 1982-83[1]. This

---

[1] Committee on Scottish Affairs, Scottish Office Memos on Expenditure 15.6.81 and 16.6.82

contrasts with the treatment of the publicly owned association, the Scottish Special Housing Association, which was treated as severely as the local authorities, and indeed more severely in 1982-83. The favourable treatment accorded did not satisfy the private associations, who proved adept at representing the increases as cuts, on the grounds that their projects, as they built up, involved an even higher rate of expenditure, and if this was denied some projects would have to be cut out entirely. They received a share of the windfall early in 1982 due to the high public receipts from the sale of council houses, and the indications are that they will continue to get special government consideration. They had even been exempted, under the Tenants' Rights Act, from the obligation to sell houses to tenants, though by 1982 Ministers, disappointed by the "wholly negative stance" of some of the associations, were putting pressure on them to sell more readily.

Looking at the public sector as a whole, there is no doubt that the Conservative government's policy on housing cuts has been directed less against capital programmes than against revenue grants and rents, to which we now turn.

HOUSING SUPPORT GRANT AND POLICY ON RENTS

The Tories inherited from Labour a system of government revenue grants which suited their policies. This was the Housing Support Grant, by which Bruce Millan's administration replaced the former system of subsidies in 1978. Introducing the Housing (Financial Provisions) (Scotland) Bill, he described it as a major step in implementing the Green Paper strategy, and said that the new grant was designed to secure fairness of distribution, to provide for adaptability, and to disengage the central government from detailed oversight of local authorities' house-building proposals. Previously every change in the subsidy system to meet new circumstances required a new Housing Bill: in future the Secretary of State, after consultation with COSLA, would determine what housing authorities' total needs were, how much income they could reasonably expect from rents, and would offer government grant equivalent to the difference. This would be distributed according to a formula which was also to be discussed with COSLA.

The Labour Government's motive was to get rid of anomalies in the old subsidy system and replace it with one where the payments to local authorities were based on objective factors such as the loan charges to be repaid, the cost of maintenance and administration of the housing stock, and the income to be expected from rents, all of which, it was thought, could be agreed in discussion with COSLA. It was a generous system, under which the Government would make up the whole of the deficit. Ultimately however it was for the government of the day to determine what the act called 'local income capacity', that is the Scottish total of rents and contributions from the rates which it thinks local authorities can reasonably charge, and this point was recognised by one or two Labour back-benchers, who feared the power that the Bill would put in the hands of any future Conservative Secretary of State. Their gloom was justified. Bruce Millan, in his HSG Order for 1979, issued in December 1978, assumed that local contributions as a whole would rise broadly in line with earnings, leaving it to councils to decide how to split the increase between rents and rates. But George Younger's 1980 Order, a year later, said bluntly that the increases required in local contributions should come mainly from rents, and that rents should rise by £1.37 to £1.40 a week to achieve this. A year later still, in January 1981, councils had raised rents on average only by 95p to do this, and the 1981 Order said that they should make up the shortfall, as well as meet the year's expected increases in costs, out of rents. This would require an average increase of £2.33 in rents per week. (The Secretary of State for the Environment was meanwhile stipulating a £2.95 increase in England.) On each occasion - under Labour as well as under the Conservatives - the HSG system enabled the Government to determine how much, in its own view, it was reasonable to pay out of national funds towards housing, whereas under the old system it was powerless to prevent subsidies changing in accordance with the statutory formulae then in force. The Conservatives made full use of this: for 1982-83 Housing Support Grant was reduced by 20% from the previous year, and as this made no allowance for inflation the cut was effectively even higher than that. By the end of 1982 it was being forecast that almost half the housing authorities would not receive any grant for 1983-84 onwards.

But though the Government could limit its direct expenditure by fixing the amount of Housing Support Grant, it could not by this means alone prevent councils ignoring the Government's rent objectives and making good the deficit out of the rates. This is because the HSG system does not allow the Secretary of State to dictate how increases shall be set as between rents and rates, whatever HSG Orders may state as to what the Government thinks desirable. Clearly the Conservative Government needed another weapon to enforce its policy; otherwise, given the reluctance of most councils to raise rents adequately, the shortfall would be likely to grow year by year and the rent increases demanded by the Government more and more unrealistic. The weapon adopted was more subtle than the statutory methods adopted by the Conservative Government of 1970-74. It was simply to make capital allocations to individual local authorities dependent on their level of rate fund contributions. This required no battle to get a Bill through Parliament, and utilised the established right of the Secretary of State to fix capital allocations. All previous administrations had determined capital allocations, based on what the government of the day thought the economy could afford and the needs demonstrated by the local authorities. Even under Labour, the government, as part of the Public Expenditure Survey system, took account of the extent to which public expenditure on housing would be met by rent income, and from time to time put out circulars suggesting what the average increase in rents should be. Given that Labour had started in 1974 by imposing a rents freeze, and that its next priority had been to dismantle the Tory legislation which would have brought subsidies to an end, Labour-controlled councils did not take much notice of these injunctions; certainly they raised rents, but not enough to make much difference to the comparatively low proportion of costs met from rents which had been reached by 1975. Nor did they affect the size of the new building and improvement programme which the Government was prepared to authorise; in general the Labour administration in Scotland was able to authorise whatever capital expenditure local authorities could reasonably be expected to achieve (some asked for more than they could possibly achieve, but that is a different matter).

INVESTMENT IN THE ENVIRONMENT

Rents as a proportion of earnings fell from 5.1% in 1977-78 to 4.7% in 1980-81.[1] At first it seemed as if George Younger and his team would simply make good the resulting increase in contributions from the rates by cutting the aggregate capital spending to be permitted by local authorities, and share out what was left in accordance with housing needs in each area. But since the new Government was committed to a reduction in all housing expenditure, current as well as capital, this would have meant that local authorities who kept their rents low and their rates contributions to housing high would swallow up a large slice of the total expenditure on housing planned by the Government. (It is a paradox of the rules of the game as played by both parties that rates count as public expenditure, but rents do not.) Admittedly the high rates contributions would have to be paid for in higher poundages in the annual rates calculation, particularly as rates contributions to housing do not in Scotland attract government Rate Support Grant, but this did not deter councils with a low-rent philosophy. By the first half of 1980 it appeared that rates contributions were rising "at a rate which would seriously reduce the resources available for public sector building and modernisation" (as a Scottish Development Department letter to local authorities put it), and in order to maintain its planned limit on housing public expenditure (£603 million in 1980-81 against £702 million in 1979-80) the options open to the Government were to make either a general cut or selective cuts in capital expenditure. Not surprisingly they chose the latter: what is surprising is that nobody, not even the most dedicated Tory opponents of low rents and high rates, had asked them to do it before. And yet the message was simple and neatly shifted much of the blame for cuts in building and modernisation on to individual local authorities: it was "keep your rates contributions down or build fewer houses". In July 1980 each council was warned that it would receive a considerably reduced capital allocation for 1981-82, but that the Secretary of State was considering a scheme whereby increased allocations could be allowed if rates contributions did not increase as much as they had been doing. This was converted in December to a firm statement that if a local authority's rates contribution exceeded a given

---

(1) Committee on Scottish Affairs. Scottish Office Memo on Expenditure 15.6.81

figure its capital allocation for 1981-82 would be reduced by the amount of the excess. (Capital spending on improvement grants and council mortgages for owner-occupiers was, however, protected against the cuts.)

The new policy was described by Labour MPs as blackmail. COSLA claimed that it was not within the spirit of earlier assurances that capital allocations would be made on the basis of need. The Scottish Development Department replied that capital allocations would continue to be based on needs, but that increased contributions from rates had to be offset somehow, and that it was better to cut those authorities who had not complied with the Department's guidelines than to cut everybody.

The public expenditure White Paper of March 1981 confirmed the new policy, stating that "to ensure that the total planned resources for local authority housing will not be exceeded, individual authorities will receive their full capital allocation only if their rate fund contribution to their housing revenue account is kept in line with the level assumed for the Housing Support Grant Order". Most of the bigger authorities (apart from Edinburgh) failed to take heed of this, and as a result their capital allocations were cut by £35 million from what they would have been. This did not result in the average rent increase of £2.33 per week which the Government had asked for, but one of about £1.85,[1] with the result that subsidies from the rates went up, instead of remaining stationary as the Government wished. A year later local authorities were told that the acceptable level of subsidy from the rates would be 35% below the level they had budgeted for in 1981-82; if any authority exceeded the level which the Scottish Office specified, the provisional capital allocation for work on council houses in 1982-83 would be cut by the full amount of the excess. In specifying a 35% reduction the Government were adding the previous year's shortfall in rents to the further reduction demanded for 1982-83; as in the case of general rate-borne expenditure they were refusing to wipe the slate clean each year. Although the policy was bitterly attacked (and received front page newspaper treatment),

---

(1) 'Rating Review, Scotland, 1981-82' (C.I.P.F.A.)

INVESTMENT IN THE ENVIRONMENT

Scottish Office Ministers pointed out that council rents were still much lower than in England, despite comparable earnings. How long such a policy can be maintained in view of the reluctance of councils to achieve the Government's targets for rents remains to be seen, but the average increase in rents which the Government set as the target for 1983-84 was rather less than before - about £1.20. The failure of a local authority to comply will rebound on its house-building and improvement programme, while the Government maintains intact its objectives on public expenditure. Its position here is much stronger than in the field of rates in general, where local authorities' resistance to Government policies results in a rise in rates and hence on what is classed as public expenditure. The outside observer might comment wryly that there ought to be room for some compromise between the Government's determination to keep rates down and the local authorities' reluctance to put rents up. The net result of the conflict of policy so far (to the end of 1982) has been a continuing reduction in the number of public sector houses built, while the number improved, although recently keeping up, has not returned to the high levels of the 1970s. [1]

TENANTS' RIGHTS

We have seen that under Tory philosophy the most important right of a council tenant is to be able to buy the house he or she lives in. That was not what was meant however by "tenants' rights" during most of the 1970s. What it then meant was whether council tenants should have security of tenure guaranteed by law, and on what terms, and whether the power of councils to impose rules on tenants' conduct and activities should be restricted. There was a good deal of criticism of tenancy conditions: for example, the Scottish Consumer Council in a report issued in 1977 said that many conditions were outdated, needlessly restrictive, incomprehensible, or misleading. The Labour Government's Green Paper of that year supported the Council's proposals for a model tenancy agreement eliminating irksome and unnecessary rules, and giving increased freedom for tenants to carry out improvements, take in lodgers, and have more scope for involvement

---

(1) Cmnd 8789

in management of their houses. Somewhat more cautiously, the Green Paper said that the Government saw no basic justification for any appreciable difference between the rights of public and private tenants to security of tenure, but thought that this would need careful working out. This sort of thinking was unwelcome to the majority of local authorities, some of whom had adopted an autocratic style of managing their housing estates; in particular they resisted legal security of tenure, maintaining they only evicted tenants when the public good required it. These attitudes were to be found among Labour and Tory Councils alike. Glasgow had some of the toughest management and transfer rules, Edinburgh more evictions, size for size. But the Labour administration pressed ahead, with little positive support within their own party, in fact outright condemnation of the Green Paper as a whole, as has been described. Hugh Brown announced that there would be legislation for a tenants' charter in the 1979-80 session of Parliament, not however including statutory security of tenure for council tenants, in deference to the objections of Scottish local authorities. With an election impending, and the Secretary of State for the Environment promising security of tenure in England, this line could not be held, and security of tenure was promised in February 1979. Though Labour lost the election, the "tenants' charter" was one of the fields in which the change of government made no difference, in fact the Tory administration joyfully adopted most of the previous administration's proposals (which at national level were entirely in accordance with Tory policy), tacked on the right-to-buy, and were consequently able to christen the whole package as the Tenants' Rights (Scotland) Bill instead of an unexciting Housing Bill, in spite of orthodoxy and Whitehall. At first, however, George Younger's team did not commit itself to granting security of tenure, so strong was the claim of local authorities that this would be a charter for the anti-social tenant. There was some talk about putting on the tenant the onus of proving that there were no grounds for repossession, which alarmed organisations like Shelter, but when the Bill was published it offered virtually complete security, subject only to carefully defined reasons for repossession which would have to be accepted by a court, such as rent arrears, neglect, or annoyance to other householders. It appeared that while the Government was prepared to listen to local authorities, it would not stay until the end of the conversation. In view of the Labour leadership's advocacy of making local authorities prove their case for repossession in court it cannot be said that the Government was acting in a partisan way, but setting the council tenant free clearly counted for more than setting the local authorities free from Government control, which the Tories had emphatically promised. In other respects too the Bill gave council tenants similar rights to private tenants - the right of succession within the family, the right to challenge unreasonable conditions of tenancy, the right to take in lodgers, the right to make improvements.

About the only Labour proposal on the management of council houses which was jettisoned by the Conservatives was a Government-financed scheme to improve house management, the quality of which had been soundly criticised in a report by the Scottish Housing Advisory Committee.(1) The Committee's recommendation that a Scottish national council should be set up to establish a high standard of qualification in housing management was endorsed by the Green Paper and put into the Labour administration's Bill, but was sacrificed to the new Government's public expenditure policies. Both parties wanted better housing management; it was generally felt that this would not come about unless the Government paid the cost of centralised training, but that was not enough to persuade the Tories to devote money to it, when their priorities were the right to buy, and secondly security of tenure. The local authorities were not particularly keen on new training arrangements, and however much tenants suffered from bad management practices they were not very vocal about it, so there was no great opposition to the change in policy.

Some other management policies advocated in the Green Paper were not rejected by the Tories, but not actively pursued - for example, that more money should be spent on management relative to other things, and that rents should reflect the relative popularity of different types of houses or locations. Anxious to cut the size of the civil service, the Conservatives could not be expected to authorise the additional staff necessary

---

(1) Training for Tomorrow - an Action Plan for Scottish Housing, HMSO 1977

to preach these policies and win converts to them, and they are not topics which greatly attract the interest of the public, the newspapers, and MPs. What does attract attention is the number of vacant council houses in some areas; but there is no easy way of filling them if applicants refuse to accept them at the rents at which they are offered or if they are in areas where misuse, vandalism, and inadequate management have made living almost intolerable. There is no quick or easy solution, but differential rents and more money spent on management might well contribute to one.

ALLOCATION POLICIES FOR COUNCIL HOUSES

Should governments have a policy on the way in which councils should allocate houses, and should they enforce it? Until 1980, the answer must be that if governments did have a policy they were unwilling to enforce it. It is too early to say whether the change which took place in 1980 is significant, but it certainly offers an interesting study on the formulation of policies in the Scottish political scene, the more so because the Scottish Office followed a different course from that adopted in England.

Governments have, since council houses began to be built, placed very few injunctions on local authorities as to how they were to allocate them to different categories of tenants. On the contrary, the powers and duties of local authorities in regard to housing were extended in 1949 from the 'working classes' to all members of the community. Statute requires local authorities to give preference to those who are overcrowded, in sub-standard houses, displaced by compulsory purchase, or (in circumstances very carefully defined) homeless or liable to become homeless. Apart from that local authorities have full discretion as to what sort of applicants they will consider.

To judge by three reports issued over a period of 30 years by the Scottish Housing Advisory Committee, local authorities have on the whole exercised that discretion pretty narrowly. One of the commonest restrictions was the refusal to let houses to those who did not live in the area; applicants had to have lived in the area for a specified length of time before their case could

could be considered. Many other exclusions were applied to a verying extent - exclusion by age (in one case up to 40), exclusion of some or all owner-occupiers, exclusion of those with more than a certain income, and the refusal to consider separated couples until a separation order or divorce was obtained.

These restrictions on eligibility for council houses no doubt arose in the first place from acute shortage of houses after the 1939-45 war, and the need to give preference to those for whom councils felt they had the greatest responsibility. But they bore little relation to actual housing needs, and were criticised time after time for causing hardship.

Residential requirements were in a different class from other restrictions. The latter could be regarded as matters for local decision; if the electorate supported a party which wanted to exclude those under 30, or those who were already owner-occupiers, then this was the democratic decision for the area, and it affected nobody else. But residential requirements did affect other areas, and indeed the country as a whole, by making it difficult or impossible for people to get a house in another area if they wished to move in search of a job or to be near relatives. As far as council houses were concerned, Scotland, even after the reorganisation of local government, was split into fifty or more city-states, with frontier controls between them. Limited schemes for allocating houses to 'key' workers, who were essential to get an industry started or keep it going, were in operation in most areas, but even with the addition of the houses provided by the Scottish Special Housing Association for economic expansion they covered only a small proportion of those who needed to move as job opportunities changed and families grew up. Council houses were being tacitly regarded as a local resource, to be allocated to local inhabitants, notwithstanding the large proportion of their costs being met by national taxes. There was vehement local opposition to access to an area's council houses being made any wider, and in particular it was argued that this would lead to the more favoured areas being swamped with applications. But the system meant that the mobility of labour was severely restricted, that industrial growth and adaptation was discouraged, and that structural unemployment - people stuck in areas of declining industries - was increased.

SCOTTISH HOUSING POLICIES

The SHAC report of 1967 'Allocating Council Houses' had advocated an end to residential qualifications, but in a dozen years very little had happened to bring this about. The Conservative opposition, in the late 1970s, was showing growing concern over this, and Teddy Taylor promised in May 1977 that a future Tory government would set up a unit to investigate transfer and allocation policies. The response of the Labour Government was to commission another report by the SHAC, in 1978, covering much the same ground as the previous one, and in the months before the election the sub-committee responsible began to collect information and invite views.

Before it completed its work, however, something new occurred: George Younger's team decided to legislate to abolish residential qualifications. When the Tenants' Rights Bill was published it was found to provide that admission to a housing waiting list should not depend on the fact that the applicant is resident in any particular area, and it stipulated also that in the allocation of council housing, no account should be taken of the length of time for which an applicant has resided in any area. The Bill also prohibited minimum waiting-times before a house could be allocated, and required councils to publish their allocation and transfer rules. Justifying the action he was taking George Younger said that the depressing effect on the economy of restrictions on housing mobility justified overriding local discretion, but he added that the Government was doing this because it wanted to give council tenants the same freedom of movement as owner-occupiers.

This sudden decision to deal with the problems of allocation policies by legislation, after many years of inactivity, and to go well beyond any previous recommendations, was an internal government decision, since there is little evidence of outside pressure, and it was not paralleled in the English Housing Bill, which simply provided that housing authorities should have allocation rules of their own devising, and publish them. There was an immediate outcry from local authorities, chiefly because the way in which the provision was drafted meant that applicants would have a right to apply in the area of their choice without having to give any family or employment reasons, and authorities in the more popular areas thought they would be swamped. Before the committee stage of the Tenants' Rights Bill Malcolm Rifkind announced that it would be amended so as to require tenants to show that they needed to move to a new area for employment, social, or medical reasons. Provided they had such reasons, however, they were to have the same priority as tenants within the area seeking an internal transfer. This gave them adequate rights to apply for a house without stepping over the heads of local inhabitants with equal or greater housing needs. As well as dealing with restrictions on mobility, the Bill also followed the earlier recommendations of the Scottish Housing Advisory Committee in prohibiting local authorities from imposing minimum ages for applicants (so long as they were over 18) or income limits, and prohibited the practice of some local authorities in holding a deserted or divorced wife (or husband, for that matter) responsible for previous debts on a house.

These provisions were accepted by Scottish MPs with little debate; probably most of them were aware from their postbags of the injustices which needed to be remedied. The Scottish Housing Advisory Committee found that most of their work had been done for them, but published a report welcoming the changes, and making useful recommendations on other aspects of house-letting policy.

To be effective, the new statutory requirements needed to be incorporated in individual councils' house-letting regulations. When these were published, as provided by the Tenants' Rights Act, it emerged that virtually every authority had incorporated the bans on residential qualifications, age and income limits, and minimum waiting periods, and repeated the statement in the Act that where an applicant had employment, social or medical reasons for going to a particular area he or she should be admitted to the waiting list. But only a small number of authorities gave these applicants the same rights as tenants seeking a transfer in their own council area, or incorporated some other arrangements for giving them their statutory rights. The great majority of authorities failed to translate these rights into practical house-letting regulations, and it will be a difficult matter for applicants to insist on the equal treatment to which they are entitled until the regulations are changed. In all probability there will be a lengthy period of persuasion and pressure before council tenants are able to move around Scotland to the full extent that the Act envisages.

POLICY TOWARDS OWNER-OCCUPIERS

All through this period the public sector in housing - council, new town, and Scottish Special Housing Association houses - was becoming less dominant in the Scottish scene, especially as regards new houses built. In 1978, for the first time, more houses were built by the private sector than the public sector: in 1979 the proportion was almost two to one. Given the very high proportion of public sector houses in the housing stock as a whole, this did not make much difference to the overall percentages and Malcolm Rifkind was wont to point out that there was more private ownership in many Eastern Bloc countries than in Scotland. Throughout the 1970s there was discussion on relatively non-partisan lines of ways in which house-purchase might be made easier, particularly by young people and others buying houses for the first time. Established owners were not thought to require any special assistance; the gradual rise in mortgage rates was not felt as severely by them, since their loans had been taken out at times of lower house prices, while first-time buyers had not only to pay rapidly rising prices but to pay higher interest on bigger loans. Special incentives for first-time buyers began to be talked about, and a section of the Labour Green Paper was devoted to this. It advocated a variety of ways in which help could be given - by getting building societies to offer more mortgages on the basis of low repayments in the early years, by arranging higher percentage mortgages, and by encouraging building society loans on older houses. This met with no opposition, and was criticised, if at all, for being inadequate. Shelter, for example, an outspoken critic of tax relief on the higher mortgages, wanted it to be reduced in order to provide more funds for first-time buyers, and professional bodies such as the Scottish Branch of the Institute of Housing criticised the savings bonus scheme as inadequate. The Labour Government, in both the English and Scottish Green Papers, had reviewed the question of tax relief, and come out in favour of making no change. It was however very active - more active than the Tory Government decided to be - in promoting the interests of owner-occupiers by maintaining a dialogue with the building societies about the level of mortgage interest and the flow of funds.

The Home Purchase Assistance Bill, introduced early in 1978, set up a scheme based on the Green Papers, offering an interest-free loan of £600 and a tax-free bonus of £110 to people who had been saving with a building society for two years. Even at the time this was a very cautious beginning, and given the escalation of house prices it cannot be said to have made more than a marginal difference to the problems of first-time buyers. It might have been thought that the Conservative Government, to promote owner-occupation, would have extended the scheme quite considerably, especially as their monetary policy led to even higher interest rates. But this would have meant more public expenditure, and in the conflict between housing policy and monetary policy it was the latter which prevailed. No further schemes were introduced to help either owner-occupiers as a whole or first-time buyers. Although it was a Conservative doctrine that the long-term benefits of monetarist policy outweighed the sacrifices which would have to be made in the short term, it is somewhat surprising that they maintained their laissez-faire policy in regard to mortgage rates, given the increasing interest rates, and the importance which they attached to expanding owner-occupation. In one respect, they changed the law in a way unfavourable to owner-occupiers who obtained a loan from a local authority, by prohibiting fixed-interest loans. The momentum of private house-building in Scotland was checked, perhaps because of growing unemployment among house purchasers as much as the high interest rates of 1979-81, falling from over 14,000 completions in 1979 to 10,000 in 1981. In any event, the situation was dominated by policies pursued by the Government for Britain as a whole; without devolution, there was not thought by either government to be scope for separate Scottish policies in this field, and even under devolution the possibilities of giving massive help to first-time buyers would have been limited by their cost.

PRIVATELY-RENTED HOUSES

By the 1970s, houses let by private landlords had been reduced to a remnant of the vast stock of houses for rent which a generation earlier had provided homes for the majority of the population. Given the system of security of tenure (even unto the third generation) and statutory fixing of rents at levels well below a commercial return on the investment, landlords had been selling whenever they had a right to do so, on the death or departure of the last statutory tenant. By and large, the houses still rented from private landlords consisted of tenements in poor and deteriorating condition, 70% of them dating from before 1919. This is not the place for a discussion of whether the policies which had led to this situation were wise or had envisaged their consequences, since we are concerned with policy changes from the 1970s onwards, and there is little evidence, even from the Tory party, of any intention to make a fundamental change in the system. The Conservative manifestos of 1974 and 1979 promised to continue security of tenure for tenants, and this of course precluded the establishment of a free market between those who had a house and those who were in search of one, particularly as 'fair rents' had to be fixed on the manifestly artificial assumption that supply equalled demand in all areas. The Labour government of 1974 extended security to tenants of furnished houses, ending an abuse but at the same time reinforcing the tendency of landlords to sell as soon as they could get vacant possession, and this was not reversed by the Tories.

Policy towards privately rented houses has therefore been, in recent years, concerned with marginal changes. In 1977 the government, both in England and Scotland, published lengthy consultative documents about a review of the Rent Acts, which had generated an exceedingly complicated system of case law. These declared a willingness to consider any change in the law, provided it was consistent with the principle of security of tenure, and suggested a series of questions for consideration on methods of fixing rents, procedure for repossession and other topics.

While consultation on the review was in progress, Bruce Millan's Green Paper on Scottish Housing was published This conceded that rent fixing arrangements are a factor affecting landlords' decisions whether to relet when a vacancy occurs (which is putting it mildly, though even so it was a bold thing for a Labour administration to say), but put the issue aside until the Rent Acts review was completed. The Green Paper did however go on to say that difficulty and delay in owners getting repossession of parts of their houses which they had let off, or of houses let temporarily during the owners' absence, deterred people from letting, and promised to do something about it.

The Green Paper also sketched a far-sighted proposal for getting new investment into privately-rented housing. It recognised that the central problem was the low rate of return from private renting and the uncertainty about future changes in the law - in other words, the feeling of property owners that they could not rely on retaining any rights as to rent and repossession which they might be granted. This suspicion seemed to be justified two or three years later by the threat of the Labour party to repeal the Tories' system of short tenancies when they regained power, but in 1977 what the Green Paper envisaged was that assurances about adequate rent increases in the long term could be given to a publicly accountable letting-agency, which would be established to provide houses at relatively high rents for those needing mobility.

Under Labour these modest proposals for changes in the law relating to private renting came to nothing. Like much else in the Green Paper, they were resented and opposed by many traditional Labour supporters. The Transport and General Workers Union saw them as an example of the "wasteful and immoral" practice of treating housing as a commodity instead of a social service. Otherwise the consultations were allowed to drag on, while the Scottish Office concentrated on other aspects of housing, and the parties prepared for the general election of 1979.

The Conservative manifesto for that election drew attention to the deterrent effect of legislation on private letting, but apart from a number of minor changes in the landlord-tenant relationship its only novel proposal was the system of shorthold tenure for short fixed terms "free from the most discouraging provisions of the present law". The Tories could not take the risk of extending this to the whole of the privately rented sector, and promised that it would not affect the position of existing tenants. Thus an ingenious system of increasing the supply of privately rented houses, when the effect of the bulk of existing legislation was to make that supply shrink, was virtually limited to cases where statutory tenants died or left of their own accord; and there was nothing to encourage landlords to relet rather than to sell, as they had been doing for the past thirty years. Even so the proposal was fiercely attacked, both inside and outside Parliament, and the Labour opposition threatened to repeal it when they regained power. The threat of repeal can be particularly effective in stultifying such a measure, since property owners could find that their short-term tenants had been given unlimited security of tenure by another change in the law. A further limitation on the new system was that short tenancies had to be registered at a 'fair rent' determined by rent officers or rent assessment committees - a concession designed, unsuccessfully, to get all-party support for the scheme. In most cases the figure fixed was likely to be well below a freely-negotiated rent or what the owner would consider an adequate return on his capital. This limitation was moreover maintained in Scotland when it was abandoned in England and Wales late in 1981.

The higher return to owners from selling rather than renting, the cost of landlords' repairs, growing dereliction and the uncertain prospects for any system of short tenancies seem likely to accelerate the decline in the number of houses available for private letting. The consequence will be that people who need to move as their jobs, opportunities and careers develop will increasingly have to choose between buying a house, if they can, and waiting for a council house.

HOUSING THE HOMELESS

In view of the shortage of housing which has persisted for so many years, despite three decades of massive house-building programmes since the Second World War, it is surprising that the plight of those who do not have a house at all failed to attract much public interest until the late sixties. Then, largely owing to the activities of a very effective pressure group, Shelter, and an influential television programme, 'Cathy come home', it gradually came to public attention that although local authorities had a general power and duty to meet the housing needs of the community as a whole, neither they nor anybody else had a specific duty to help particular unfortunates who had no place where they could legitimately live, and were in real danger of being put out on to the street. In the course of time the cry went up all over Britain that something should be done for them, and it is the purpose of this section to show what the response was in Scotland, and how far the policies adopted differed from those in England and Wales.

It was not unanimously accepted that homelessness was a housing problem at all. Many housing authorities argued that families or individuals got into a situation where they were put out or about to be put out of wherever they had been living as a result of social problems and that it was for social work authorities to advise them and provide for them. A less extreme point of view was that the responsibility must be shared, but that if housing authorities had a statutory duty to provide houses for such people they would in effect have to shoulder the whole responsibility. The dissension between those who held that view and those who maintained that housing authorities must be given a statutory duty towards the homeless was one of the main reasons for the delay in legislation being passed and the further delay, especially in Scotland, in framing a code of practice for the administration of the law by local authorities.

At an early date it was realised in the Scottish Office that the impending reorganisation of local government would make matters worse, by splitting responsibilities for housing and for social work, over the whole of mainland Scotland, between district and regional councils respectively, whereas previously, in the cities at least, the city corporations were responsible for both topics. A committee chaired by Mrs J Morris was set up in 1973 to consider this problem, and its report issued in 1975(1), emphasised the common interest of housing and social work services in many areas of local activity, and criticised the unhelpful or even damaging attitudes which existed, one side accusing the other of being more interested in getting rent than with the welfare of tenants, and being accused in turn of sacrificing the interests of the majority of tenants to those of anti-social tenants. The Morris committee made a special study of homelessness (a field in which it found co-

---

(1) 'Housing and Social Work - a joint approach' HMSO 1975

operation was particularly bad), and set a useful example - not always followed by others - in distinguishing between those who were actually roofless or about to become so, and those who were inadequately housed. It expressed itself as 'basically in favour of the proposition that the primary responsibility for housing the homeless should in future rest with housing authorities'.

This recommendation was rejected by the housing authorities, and Scottish Ministers took the line that the problem should be resolved by discussion and co-operation. The Secretary of State for the Environment was meanwhile saying that the Government could not find time for a Bill of their own, but would support a private member's Bill. Such a Bill was introduced early in 1977 by Stephen Ross, and it applied to Scotland. At the second reading, in February, Scottish Ministers were still opposed to legislation in Scotland, and Hugh Brown said he hoped the sponsor of the Bill would delete Scotland from it, because the objective should be reached by agreement among the different local authorities. This vain hope would have put off a decision indefinitely. At this point, however, the Scottish Office line was changed by an event in the wider political field, namely the vanishing majority of Labour at Westminster and the need to conclude a pact with the Liberals. One of the terms of this was legislation on homelessness; Hugh Brown announced in March that he would review his position on the Bill, and no more was heard about excluding Scotland from it. The resistance of housing authorities to legislation was thus set aside as a result of a political crisis at Westminster.

In the meantime the Bill itself had been amended a good deal, in particular by distinguishing between priority categories of the homeless, who had to be given a house, and non-priority categories, who were entitled to temporary accommodation or just to advice. Another important change was that those who were 'intentionally homeless' (which included those being evicted for rent arrears) were to have no rights to accommodation. Thirdly, the 'local connections' of applicants had to be decided, and an elaborate procedure for deciding which local authority was responsible, reminiscent of the nineteenth-century poor law, was created. These were radical changes, which were strongly opposed, but were probably the only means by which a well-intentioned Bill could be turned into a practicable Act. If homelessness, irrespective of the circumstances, had given a right to a house, sensible priority schemes run by councils would have been destroyed; and if eviction for rent arrears - with the permission of a court - had not been possible in the last resort, arrears would have mounted intolerably. But severe social problems, such as the problems of the single homeless and of those who were permanently excluded from council housing because of rent arrears, were left unsolved.

Scottish considerations played little part in determining the form which the Act eventually took, and in this respect it does not offer much of a field for discussion of how policies in Scotland are determined (except as regards the effect of Westminster politics on applying the Bill to Scotland). But what happened after the Act became law - or rather what for a long time did not happen - illustrates rather well the forces which affect the making of Scottish policy.

Housing authorities had been given responsibility for providing for the homeless within the limited terms of the Act, but recognising that this would not end the matter the Act required them to have regard to guidance given by the Secretary of State. It was on this that Shelter and the other organisations concerned pinned their hopes of securing a generous interpretation of housing authorities' responsibilities. In England and Wales, a code of guidance(1) was issued without much delay. A good deal of this was simply an explanation of the Act, but it emphasised the need for quick and sympathetic consideration of applications by homeless people, and there was a valuable annex on the prevention of homelessness by action at early stages, including early attention to households in arrears with their rent.

In an attempt to bring together the housing and the social work authorities, who were still in bitter disagreement, the Act had provided for the code of guidance in Scotland to be drawn up by a local authority working party, subject to the agreement of the Secretary of State, and the date for bringing the Act into operation

(1) HMSO November 1977

was put off until 1 April 1978, four months later than in England and Wales. But extra time was not enough. As the months passed, it became clear that the two factions in COSLA institutionalised in the Housing and the Social Work Committees, were not going to reach agreement, and the Scottish Development Department began to realise that it would have to issue its own circular. But what should it say? Scottish Ministers were not prepared to overrule the COSLA Housing Committee by writing a code of guidance themselves or adopting the English code as the formal statutory guidance. The local authority working party had agreed that the English code should be 'commended to the attention' of local authorities, but such was the standing given to the views of the housing authorities that even this was watered down, and the eventual circular [1] issued in February 1978 simply said that authorities "may wish to consult" the English code (blandly described as "a useful description of the provisions of the Act").

The circular did contain two paragraphs of formal guidance about the quick, confidential and sympathetic treatment of applications from the homeless and the need to give applicants the benefit of the doubt whether their homelessness was intentional; it urged authorities to take early remedial action, not to split households, and to take into account an applicant's views on what his local area was. Above all, it advised close co-operation between housing and social work authorities. The pressure groups for the homeless gave no credit to the Department for its attempt to take some action in spite of the rift among local authorities and described the circular as "useless and damaging". [2] The Press, in some quarters, recognised that the Department was "trying to steer a middle course instead of wielding the big stick", [3] and that the reason for what had happened was the failure of COSLA to reach agreement within itself.

How necessary for the proper working of the Act was a code of guidance? The pressure groups continued to castigate the Government for not producing one, and the district councils for failing in sympathy with the

---

(1) Circular No. SDD 13/1978
(2) 'The Scotsman', 23.2.1978
(3) Ibid, 3.3.1978

homeless. It was claimed that they were classifying 15% to 20% of applicants as intentionally homeless, as against 4% in England; the official figures for the first 18 months[1] were 12% at first dropping to 8% later. The district councils, however, could point to the same figures to show that out of 7,010 applicants whom they assessed as being unintentionally homeless and in one of the priority categories they had provided permanent accommodation for 5,822 and short stay accommodation for 1,020. Corresponding figures for priority applicants threatened with homelessness were 2,841, of whom 1,795 got permanent and 589 temporary accommodation. In addition the district councils could point out that they offered permanent accommodation to nearly half of those whom they classed as intentionally homeless, provided they were among the priority categories. A quarter of the applicants were, however, assessed by councils as not having priority, and it was largely on this that the pressure groups based their criticism of the Act and the local administration of it.

There was criticism from the other direction, of course: the housing convener of Edinburgh was reported as saying that the Act would also allow people to get free holidays in Edinburgh, and other political figures questioned why "someone out of the blue" should be given precedence, although it is difficult to see how either event could come about under the Act in the form in which it became law. There was more substance in the criticism that the Government expected the Act to be operated without an increase in total expenditure, in spite of the fact that some families were given specific rights to housing which they did not possess before. But they amounted to only about 1% of families living in council houses, and the Government maintained that they could be given houses from the existing stock of council property. In a few cases local authorities were taken to court for alleged failure to observe the Act, but while this generated a good deal of publicity it did not substantially affect the operation of the Act one way or another.

The Labour government refused to be pushed into dictating a code of practice, and arranged a joint working party with COSLA. This painstakingly worked out a compromise report, and after some tortuous negotiations between the Housing and Social Work Committees COSLA was able

(1) Scottish Housing Statistics No. 9, HMSO 1980

to submit a single agreed view on it in May 1979. This put the newly elected team at the Scottish Office in a position to say they would issue a code of practice in the light of experience of the first year's operation of the Act, and work on this went ahead while accusations and counter-accusations continued to fly about - district councils being charged with trying to 'dump' the homeless, while one councillor, sitting on the other side of the fence, claimed that houses set aside for the homeless were being used as brothels.

Not until September 1980 was the long-awaited code of practice published. It turned out to be almost identical to the English code, and it is difficult to see why there had been so much resistance to adopting the latter. Introducing it, Malcolm Rifkind claimed that in the two years that the Act had been in operation housing authorities had operated it in a humane and reasonable manner, 13,000 households having been given permanent and 6,000 temporary accommodation, out of 27,000 applicants, of whom 17,000 were assessed by the authorities as being in a priority category. Although these figures are not denied, the pressure groups concerned with the homeless continue to assert that the problem is very far from being solved, and it remains to be seen whether they can obtain changes in policy, particularly in the interests of categories such as families who are in rent arrears through inability to manage their affairs, and those of the single homeless who require special guidance in order to sustain a tenancy. The Act allows the government to change the priority categories, and it is on this that the pressure groups must pin their hopes.

HOUSING POLICY - SOME GENERAL CONCLUSIONS

Few public issues illustrate as well as housing the circumstances which determine Scottish policies, and the influence of different agencies on the process. It is a subject of great importance in itself; it has been accepted for sixty years or more as a proper field for government participation and responsibility; it generates a great flow of comments and statements both locally and nationally; it is politically contentious; and it is an area in which there is a long tradition

(1) SDD September 1980 (not HMSO)

of separate Scottish legislation and administrative measures. Also significant is the fact that it is a mixed sector of the economy, partly public; partly private, with different policy requirements for each, and differing contributions, over the years, to the needs of the people of Scotland.

If housing is an area in which governments are expected to take action, what determines and limits their power to act? The first determinant is party policy as expressed in manifestos and in major undertakings given while out of office. For many years there was virtual unanimity in party statements that what was needed was a bigger and more effective public housing programme, but by the beginning of the seventies disputes as to how it should be paid for began to predominate, and what had to a large extent been a bipartite policy had been cleft by the arguments about subsidies and rents, and subsequently even more by the Tory commitment to give tenants the right to buy their council houses. Yet statements of party policy with regard to the private sector remained basically similar: all parties wanted more private house-building and none wanted to upset the security of tenure of the tenants of private landlords of the 'fair rent' system. The Labour governments of 1974 onwards made it their first priority to stop the dismantling of the subsidy system instituted by the Tories, but apart from that were committed to previous policies: it was only later that new policy ideas were to be discussed in the Housing Green Paper of 1977.

The Tories, for their part, committed themselves specifically by their 1979 manifesto to the policies which they have since pursued, and to which in the main they have been able to give effect because of their secure majority at Westminster. The contrast between this and the difficulty which Bruce Millan's administration had to retain the backing of Labour back-benchers is marked. At most times, back-bench support is of more importance to a government than the attitude of Opposition parties. Very rarely does a government change its policy because of Opposition parliamentary questions or Opposition motions, and if an Opposition back-bencher wants to exert any influence he must choose topics outside the main party battle, or on which the government party is divided. But if a government is contemplating policies which do not have the full support of its own back-benchers it must judge carefully how far it can go before some of its supporters abstain in Parliamentary divisions or even vote against it, and how politically damaging this would be. Bruce Millan, for example, was prepared to give permission to councils to sell their houses where this would not affect the waiting list, but he could not go as far as giving a general consent, as his colleagues in England did. He could issue general exhortations to councils to keep rents in line with increases in earnings, but could not do anything to enforce this. On a larger scale, he could issue a Green Paper setting out many possible new lines of action for Labour on housing, but he could not prevent the Labour Party in Scotland from rejecting it, and had, as a consequence, to handle his back-benchers very carefully to make sure he did not have to depend on Tory votes or abstentions in the House of Commons to get through such of the Green Paper proposals as he thought it possible to make progress with.

Thus even in a period of tiny majorities (preserved in the later years of the administration only by the Lib-Lab pact) it was understandings and arrangements behind the scenes which counted rather than the Parliamentary debates themselves, which only the most innocent witness of the political scene would expect to lead to changes in policy. The situation since the 1979 election has, of course, illustrated a very different aspect of policy-making in Scotland: if sufficiently determined, a party with a majority at Westminster need pay very little attention to the views of the majority of Scottish MPs. The Conservative administration under George Younger was unaffected by the fact that the majority of Scottish MPs were opposed to its housing policies, and was able to legislate for the right to buy council houses, to cut financial allocations, and to cut the capital allocations of councils who did not raise rents adequately, without any worry about the Parliamentary consequences.

In housing the advent of the 1979 Government produced a change in attitude to public sector housing greater than that of any previous election for many years, and policies which had been followed by administrations of both parties were reversed or abandoned. The most fundamental change may prove to be not the granting of the right to buy council houses, or the creation of new five year tenancies, but the fact that funds for public sector housing ceased to be available virtually on demand, as had been the case for thirty years, and became subject to real restrictions. The promotion of housing in the public sector as a whole ceased to be a major objective of government, which concentrated its support on particular sectors such as grants to private owners and tenants and the housing associations. Housing during the post-1945 period might previously have been taken as a perfect illustration of the incremental theory, that policy changes take place only in small steps, but the 1979 changes were too radical to support this view. Even if reversed by future legislation, they may by then have transformed the nature and the image of council housing. It is paradoxical that some of the legislation which made this possible had been created by the Labour government, notably the introduction of housing support grant, and this was precisely what some Labour back-benchers had feared.

Of the other possible constraints on policy, the availability of finance has not been critical for either Government in Scottish housing affairs. Although pressed by external circumstances to keep public expenditure down, the Labour administration in Scotland was able by and large to authorise as much capital expenditure as councils needed to incur, and to provide housing support grant to make up the deficit between actual rents and actual running costs. The housing support grant system contained no incentive to local authorities to economise or obtain the best value for money spent and Labour Ministers indicated that something would have to be done about this, but nothing was done before the change of government. Then the financial considerations were reversed: it was not a question of finding money to pay for housing policies, but of how much housing could contribute to the reduction in total government expenditure. Fortunately for the new government, their most cherished policies, those enshrined in the Tenants' Rights Act, did not make any demand on public expenditure, and the Conservative policies of encouraging owner-occupation and making council tenants pay a higher proportion of total housing costs would have led to a reduction in housing expenditure even if the Government had not been looking for savings overall.

SCOTTISH HOUSING POLICIES

If financial considerations did not determine Scottish housing policy under either government then neither did English, as distinct from UK, factors enforce uniformity of policy with England except in the sense that the Tory government depended on a mainly English majority. The Labour administration in Scotland devised the housing plan system[(1)] and introduced the new system of housing support grant independently and in advance of changes in England and Wales, while money for housing continued to be provided at a higher rate per head of population. Bruce Millan maintained a different line from his English colleagues on limiting permissions to sell council houses. He was however forced by the Lib-Lab pact to come into line with England about legislation on homelessness, and by the imminence of an election to come into line on the "tenants'" charter. George Younger maintained a different line from England on house allocation rules and on the right to buy council houses in rural areas, demanded smaller rent increases and lesser housing cuts than in England and adopted a different procedure for penalising low-rent authorities.

Legislation put through by both administrations differed in detail from English legislation - sometimes important detail, such as the machinery for taking sales of council houses out of the hands of reluctant local authorities - and day-to-day administration remained as independent as it always has been. But to quote Malcolm Rifkind, "the Scottish Office ..... always follows the splendid tradition of insisting on United Kingdom uniformity when we like what our English colleagues are doing and asserting the need for distinctive Scottish solutions when we don't".[(2)]

The role of officials in formulating and modifying housing policy is, of course, confidential, by a long-standing tradition and indeed by law. The formal and actual role of senior civil servants is to advise Ministers, and they reject the allegation that they marshal their advice so as to make the decision inevitable. It was part of the Labour back-bench criticism of the Green Paper of 1977 that it indicated that officials were pressing Ministers to modify their policies faster than they wanted to, but this would be an aspersion on Bruce Millan,

---

(1) SDD Circular No. 76/1976

(2) The Scottish Government Year Book 1982 (ed. H & N Drucker)

who was not a Minister likely to be driven where he did not want to go or to be overwhelmed by the amount of detailed evidence put to him by his officials. The style of the Green Paper did however suggest that official advice to Ministers, backed up with adequate statistical information, could have an effect on Ministers whose minds were not closed to change. With the change of government, the Department found itself implementing radically different new policies, issuing a circular giving councils blanket approval to sell houses to tenants, and drafting the memoranda which eventually led to the right-to-buy provisions in the Tenants' Rights Act. Other Tory policies, particularly those which had been suggested in the 1977 Green Paper, required less of a reversal of direction.

The critic might say that civil servants should have done more to moderate radical changes, but this would be to misunderstand their function. If a party proposal is administratively impracticable, or would have unforeseen consequences, it is the duty of Ministerial advisers to say so, but not to try to enforce their views. Matters such as the proper level of investment or the proper level of rents in council housing, or whether it is right to grant council tenants the right to buy the houses they live in, are questions to be decided by Ministers.

Although local authorities are free to criticise government policies and advocate their own, events in the housing field in the last few years indicate how little power they have to resist unwelcome legislative changes. District councils were solidly against legislation on homelessness, but though they got it modified they could not stop it entirely; they resisted giving security of tenure to council tenants, without success; and though mostly opposed to having to sell council houses to tenants they had in the end to comply with the legislation.

The situation is different where local authorities are the executants of policy in their own areas. In such a situation their ability to resist government policies is much greater. Government exhortations on housing management, on co-operation with social work authorities, and on housing allocation schemes had little effect, and it remains to be seen whether legislation on the last of those topics will be effective. In regard to rents councils have similarly fallen behind government targets, Labour as much as Conservative. Thus in November 1977, Hugh Brown faced with dismay the refusal of Glasgow District Council to increase rents, and warned that this could lead to cuts in housing subsidy for every authority in Scotland (under the policy then current). But the fact that legislation is the responsibility of Parliament and the principle that local authorities are responsible for their own policies within the discretion that legislation gives them are equally important aspects of British constitutional practice, and local authorities' indifference to government advice does not necessarily prove them ill-advised or wrong.

The success of pressure groups in securing changes in housing policy has been as mixed as that of local authorities. The outstanding success was that of Shelter, which was largely responsible for changing and mobilising public opinion in favour of legislation for the homeless. Shelter could not however force local authorities or the government to adopt the massive building programme they advocated, nor did they make any impression on the Tories' determination to grant the right to buy council houses. The STUC, in spite of its close connections with the Labour party, was equally unable to get a big building programme adopted. In a more restricted field, however, the Scottish Federation of Housing Associations persuaded the Conservative government - already well disposed to them - to shield housing associations from the worst of the cuts in housing capital expenditure. COSLA, which is in any case a representative organisation rather than a normal pressure group, is more a source of advice on the administrative consequences of government policies rather than a partner in formulating those policies. In this very varied scene there is no evidence for the view that the balance of power among pressure groups determines the course of public policy: the most that can be said is that they can occasionally change public opinion and that they can, rather more often, secure fairly restricted objectives which do not conflict with major party policies.

The making of policy goes on under the scrutiny of the newspapers, radio, and television, and as mentioned earlier housing gets more attention than environmental topics. Much of the coverage is, however, of local matters - rents, treatment of tenants, 'queue-jumping', evictions, etc. - and housing policy on the national scale rarely gets the headline treatment regularly given to economic and employment questions. The disputes between the Tory government and Labour councils over rents have received only a fraction of the publicity given to the arguments over rates, although both involve a government 'claw-back' of a similar scale. Mortgage rate changes get prominent treatment, but it is doubtful whether this publicity has any effect on the financial policies of the building societies and the banks. Since the days of the agitation about legislation for the homeless, newspaper campaigns have rarely succeeded in affecting housing policy on a national scale, and in general Ministers' decisions are determined much more by their published policies - whether announced in Green Papers or party manifestos - and by the movement of opinion within their parties, than by Press, radio, or television comment.

As regards MPs, Labour Ministers in the end maintained the loyalty of the great majority of their parliamentary supporters, and Tory back-benchers have had no occasion to question the adherence of their leaders to party policies. Under neither government has finance restricted the policies adopted. Ministers, in short, have not been driven off course and have modified their policies only in minor respects in response to representations and consultations, although the value of consultation on technical and administrative matters must not be underestimated.

The second half of the 1970s witnessed two revolutions in Scottish housing policy - the Labour Green Paper and the Tory manifesto of 1979. The second almost negated the first and removed all prospect of the adoption of generally agreed policies. In the face of the Tory determination to cut the demand which public sector housing makes on public expenditure, and to force councils to sell houses to tenants, Labour resistance has taken the form of reversion to more traditional attitudes. In a situation where Labour and Conservative approaches to housing are more divided than they have been for many years, it seems fairly certain that policies will continue to be determined by traditional party principles.

CHAPTER III

TOWN AND COUNTRY PLANNING

With one major exception, town and country planning does not arouse party political controversy to anything like the same extent as housing, and discussion of planning policies therefore takes place in a very different atmosphere. The principles of planning do not figure very largely in party statements and manifestos, nor are decisions at national level usually made on party lines. The exception is in a field where there has never been any scope for distinctive Scottish policies, and after it has been examined briefly it can be excluded from further examination here.

LAND VALUES

Abstract and technical as the question of the development value of land may seem, it has deeply divided the Labour and Conservative parties since the Second World War. Labour has always taken the view that since the increase in the value of land on the prospect of development is due to growth and change in the community, the community and not the landowner should have the benefit of it. The Tory view is that trying to take away development value from the owner will remove any incentive to permit development, or result in a situation where the actual developer pays the increased value of the land twice - to the owner and to the community.

The Labour government elected in 1945 passed legislation which nationalised all development values throughout Great Britain for compensation of £300m; developers were expected to pay the whole of the development value when development took place, and the Central Land Board was created to administer this system. It did not work that way, and the Tories, who opposed and ridiculed it, abolished it when they came to power. (They did not, however, repeal the rest of the Act, which enshrined an even more radical principle, the basis of all future planning policies, that development of land requires permission, and that no compensation is payable if it is refused.) The Labour government of the 1960s introduced a modified form of this system, which was also repealed by the Tories. Labour's third attempt was rather different: basically it empowered local authorities to acquire land suitable for development, and envisaged that at a later date all land would be acquired by local authorities before it could be developed. The community would buy at existing use value and sell at development value. Unfortunately for this policy, it meant public expenditure on the acquisition of land, which had two fatal drawbacks: only a very limited amount of public expenditure could be authorised by the Labour government because of the general economic situation, and the land would be bought in advance of development and therefore show no return, perhaps for years.Those problems might have been overcome in time, but the Conservative government of 1979 did not give time: their first act was to refuse all further authorisations to buy land under the scheme, and then they repealed it entirely. All that was left of the structure created by Labour was development land tax, which collects from the landowner a substantial proportion of development value realised over £50,000, but does not prevent him adjusting his price, if he can, to recoup it from the developer.

At no period in this long saga was there any distinctive Scottish contribution, though much time was spent in the Scottish Office modifying the legislation and making regulations to ensure that policy was adapted in detail to Scottish land and planning law. It was not considered by the Labour governments that their schemes could take any different form in Scotland from England and Wales. There was not the same tradition of differing legislation in planning as in housing; whereas in housing there are a substantial number of legislative and policy variants, in planning the tradition has been to adapt English legislation. Moreover legislation concerned with development values is legislation on a kind of tax; and taxation is a UK matter. Even Labour's devolution proposals of the 1970s would have excluded legislation on development values from the powers of the Assembly. It is interesting to speculate whether any future devolution proposals would do the same, and whether any power to act separately from England would in fact be used. It is possible to conceive a situation in which land for development was bought up by local authorities and resold to developers in Scotland but not in England, but the Scottish central authority would have to fund the initial purchases, and unless the system was much more flexible than under the Community Land Act it might act as a disincentive to develop in Scotland rather than south of the Border.

REGIONAL REPORTS

Let us now turn to those aspects of planning in which there was scope for Scottish initiative.

An initiative which has attracted much favourable comment was the inclusion in the Local Government (Scotland) Act 1973 - the Act which reorganised local government into regions and districts - of a section requiring the new major authorities to prepare regional reports. This envisaged that the reports would be planning-orientated: they were to be based on surveys of the type required for development plans, and were to contain planning proposals for the region of the kind which would be found in a structure plan, that is, proposals about the development and use of land.

In what way, then, would the regional reports differ from structure plans? The answer became apparent in SDD Circular No. 4/75, of January 1975, which gave guidance on the purpose and form of the reports. This stated that regional reports would not be effective unless their physical planning content was based on policies outside the physical planning field. The regional councils should ensure that the reports should reflect their corporate policy on economic and social (as well as environmental) problems. Moreover the reports should be closely linked to financial plans. They should identify the areas in the region where positive action was required in the near future, and indicate how existing investment policies would have to be modified. With all this, the reports were to be brief and comprehensible, and got ready within a year and a half. This would be impossibly fast progress for conventional planning, but the reports were not to be subject to the lengthy process of advertisement, objection, and public inquiry, which applies to development plans. Essentially they were to be reports on the regional councils' policies, and the only procedures to which they were to be subject were, firstly, consultation with the district councils during preparation, and, when they were complete, submission to the Secretary of State, who was not required to approve or modify them, but simply give his response to them.

The new regional councils welcomed the opportunity to state their corporate policies in the first year or so of their existence, and responded by preparing regional reports which to a remarkable degree complied with the Secretary of State's guidance, and were in the main completed within a few months of the deadline he set. Perhaps they offered planning committees and officials the opening they had been wanting for years, to take the lead in formulating plans covering not only proposals for the use of land (the formal town and country planning function), but co-ordinating other local authority functions such as economic development; roads, traffic, and transportation; housing; and services such as water and sewerage. Although in some cases the coverage of issues such as education and social work was cursory, the regional reports as a whole met the requirement that they should deal with economic and social matters as well as environmental issues.

The responses issued by the Scottish Office to each report generally indicated agreement with the key issues identified and the means of dealing with them. Only occasionally were reservations expressed - for example, about the size of the future population of Glasgow for which it was realistic to plan - and although it had been stated that local authorities should not assume increased levels of public funding the Scottish Office did not in general have to take issue on their proposals for expenditure. It was fortunate both for the local authorities and the Scottish Office that formal approval of the reports was not required, since this removed most of the formality connected with a structure plan and allowed the local authorities to draft and the Scottish Office to comment more freely. The local authorities may have felt in some cases that the Scottish Office responses were less than comprehensive, and did not match the amount of work put into preparing the reports but they were reports on council, not government, policy, and it would have been out of place to do more than comment on the main issues in the reports, and indicate whether the Secretary of State would be able to give complete or qualified support if matters came to him for decision.

In the course of the next three or four years, during which the regional reports received a good deal of commendation elsewhere in the UK and abroad as a successful venture into corporate planning, the question began to be asked whether the exercise would be repeated. One council - Central - produced a revised regional report on its own initiative in 1979, and the Scottish Development Department took soundings on whether a general direction to prepare a second round of reports would be acceptable. There was a good deal of support for the idea, as the corporate plan contained in the first reports had proved a good base for constructive action.

Nevertheless there were considerable difficulties in inviting a second round. The empowering section in the Local Government Act, as we have seen, required reports to be based on planning surveys, and the clear implication was that they were to be preliminary to the structure plans required under the Town and Country Planning Acts. By 1979 most structure plans were either recently completed, or at an advanced stage, and it did not seem possible to insist on regional authorities submitting a report on their policies when most of those policies had been, or were about to be, formally set out in the structure plan. It also seemed unlikely that in these circumstances the Scottish Office could once again insist on an interpretation of the regional report idea which went beyond the terms of statute, where it was an adjunct of the planning of land use. Furthermore, the earliest date for the completion of the new regional reports would have been late 1981, six months before the next regional elections. A report by an outgoing council would lack credibility, and would in any case have to be re-examined by the new council. So the Scottish Office decided to put off a decision on a further round until after the 1982 elections.

In spite of the importance of the regional reports as major statements of council policy, they had attracted relatively little public or political attention. In few cases did public opinion, or the views of organised interests, affect the contents of the reports, and in fact no procedure was laid down for taking account of representations, apart from the requirement to consult district councils. The justification for this was that the reports were prepared by newly elected councils, and their popular mandate was sufficient warrant for them to determine and publish their policies. A statutory procedure for consultation would have meant a virtual duplication of the structure plan procedure. Nevertheless the only justifiable time for drawing up reports without public consultation and the opportunity of making representations is very shortly after an election. The period after the 1978 elections was inappropriate because of the state of work on structure plans, and whether regional reports are ever called for again probably depends on the general state of relations between local authorities and the government of the day, and whether the government wishes to invite a series of reports which are likely to advocate more public expenditure rather than less.

NATIONAL PLANNING GUIDELINES

Regional reports had been a means for setting out policies at the regional level, but did not embrace any statement of government policy, except so far as could be deduced from the Scottish Office's comments on the reports. The Scottish Office however utilised the planning system in the latter part of the seventies to set out some of the principles which planning policy would follow at the level of central government by issuing a series of National Planning Guidelines.

In the past there had been few attempts to state in advance what policy the government would follow in regard to proposals for development, or the restriction of development, which came before it, whether in approving development plans, deciding which planning applications to take over from local authorities, or deciding appeals. An attempt to do this during the sixties by designating growth areas had met so much hostility from areas not so designated that it was dropped. Moreover the orthodox view was that stating policies in advance would prejudge the Secretary of State's position as appellate authority, in which he is required to act in a quasi-judicial fashion by not making up his mind until he has heard all the evidence.

The coming of North Sea oil and gas, however, altered the situation. Industrial development in the form of onshore terminals, pipeline landfalls, treatment plants, or rig and platform construction yards was going to take place on an unprecedented scale and in considerable haste, and if this occurred without adequate pre-planning it was likely to be less than ideal from the economic and social point of view and environmentally very damaging. The evidence of the effect of unplanned industrial growth in the past on Scottish cities and Scottish countryside was all too plain, and there was general agreement that this must not be allowed to happen again. And for once it could not be argued that restrictions would lead to desirable development not taking place or taking place elsewhere than in Scotland, because the oil industry, with the support of government, was anxious to start the exploitation of the new under-sea resources as soon as possible, and the geographical advantages of Scotland were too great to be ignored.

Locally, the control of oil-related development rested with district and regional councils, but the view in the Scottish Office was that so many of the issues were of national importance that many of them would have to be determined by central government. It also followed, again in their view, that the central government should give some indication of the principles it would follow in the actions it took. The most immediate need was to draft a national policy on coastal development, since the greater part of oil-related industry needed a location on the coast for obvious reasons. In 1973 the Scottish Development Department published a discussion paper on the subject, and by August 1974, after comments had been received, this became the Coastal Planning Guideline for North Sea Oil and Gas.[1] It was based on the concepts of preferred conservation zones, in which oil-related development could be justified only in exceptional circumstances, and preferred development zones, in which

(1) SDD August 1974 (not HMSO)

development should be encouraged. The Secretary of State, it stated, expected local authorities to exercise their planning functions within this framework, and would take his own decisions within the same context, but he did not regard this as prejudging particular development applications.

The list of conservation and development zones contained few surprises; the former included the whole of the west highland coast because of its scenic and ecological importance, and the latter included not only areas such as Sullom Voe and Nigg Bay where development had already started, but also practically the whole of the Forth and Clyde estuaries, because the government saw oil-related development as hopefully a means of modernising the industrial structure of the central belt of Scotland. Every region - in the local government sense - had at least one preferred development zone in it, so that none could complain that development was being steered away from it. In the geographical sense, one very large region, the west highland coast, was denied a preferred development zone, but events were soon to change that.

The success of the guideline strategy must in fact be regarded as very mixed. Certainly the majority of oil-related developments have occurred in the preferred development zones, including one of the most potentially valuable, the Mossmorran-Braefoot Bay petrochemical complex, within the central belt, and there was one major success in steering a gas terminal away from a site of great ecological importance at the Loch of Strathbeg, in Buchan. But the integrity of the west highland conservation zone was twice breached by the need to provide sites with deep water access for oil platform construction, at Loch Kishorn and Portavadie on Loch Fyne, fruitlessly in the latter case, since it never built a platform. Furthermore the conservation zone in Lothian became the site of the Torness nuclear power station. This was not technically a breach of the guideline, since Torness is not an oil-related development, but using the same criteria such a development in such an area could be justified (in the words of the guideline) only in exceptional circumstances.

Guidelines on other national planning matters were issued in subsequent years - on Large Industrial Sites, Aggregate

Working, Rural Conservation, and Petrochemical Developments in 1977, and on the Location of Major Shopping Developments in 1978. These were supplemented in 1981 by guidelines on Land for Housing, Rural Planning Priorities, National Scenic Areas, Nature Conservation, and Forestry, and some of the earlier guidelines were revised.[1] The policy advice contained in the guidelines had meanwhile been supplemented by statutory requirements for local authorities to notify the Scottish Office if they proposed to grant permission for development contrary to the guidelines, so that the Secretary of State could consider whether to call in the application. He could thus ensure that there were no breaches of the guideline except by his own decision. But the notification procedure was also a genuine attempt to indicate to local authorities the areas in which matters would not be taken out of their hands by the Secretary of State, and those areas were increased in 1980 by withdrawal of the need to notify aggregate working, major shopping developments, and (on the introduction of National Scenic Areas) coastal development.

The concept of national guidelines was taken over by George Younger's administration with only minor changes, such as greater emphasis on the release of enterprise by good planning policies, and there was a reissue in 1981, extended by new guidelines on land for housing and the balance between development and conservation in rural areas. The series varies to a considerable extent in the strictness of the principles to be followed: thus local authorities are required not to grant planning permission for building on prime agricultural land except in accordance with approved structure and local plans or after notification to the Scottish Office, and certain named sites for large industry and for petrochemical development are protected by a similar procedure. At the other extreme, local authorities for rural areas are merely enjoined to give priority to planning those areas where competing interests are most likely to arise, and no attempt is made to state the principles on which such conflicts should be settled, other than a reminder that development in the open countryside should be frowned upon unless the local plan provides otherwise. Many topics of the greatest importance are not yet covered

---

(1) National Planning Guidelines 1981. SDD (not HMSO)

by guidelines, for example, roads and public transport planning, the design of new areas for development, the balance between new building and rehabilitation, and the location of hazardous industries. There is a good deal of guidance elsewhere on such problems not so far incorporated into guidelines, but the system can be extended, as shown by the fact that George Younger's decision on the 'Lurcher's Gully' proposal in the Cairngorms late in 1982 incorporated a plan to publish guidelines on the location of major ski-ing developments.

It therefore seems that the guidelines remain a useful policy device, not so far adopted elsewhere in the UK, to demarcate national and local planning issues, to state the broad principles which the Scottish Office will adopt in exercising its planning powers, and to suggest how local authorities should exercise theirs. The system, it must be said, owes little to public participation in framing it, and with one exception to be discussed later, has aroused little interest outside professional planning circles, but in the long run it may have more effect on the fact of Scotland and on the country's economy than many other government policies which have attracted more discussion and controversy.

THE SCOPE OF PLANNING CONTROL

At the same time as the guidelines system was being elaborated, the Scottish Development Department started a series of discussions about the scope of planning control - what the community expected of planning, whether changes should be made in the kinds of development free of planning control, and what the best arrangements were for consultation on and notification of planning applications.

A lengthy discussion document circulated in April 1977[1] posed a number of questions. Should different degrees of development control apply to different areas, according to local characteristics and preferences? Should some alternative to planning control be found for developments whose only effect was on immediate neighbours? Should planning authorities decide whether particular planning applications should be advertised? Should there be new

(1) Review of the Management of Planning. SDD 1977 (not HMSO)

arrangements for listed buildings and conservation areas? Should part of the cost of planning be recouped by charging for applications, as with applications for building consent? Should the design briefs for areas due for development or redevelopment avoid prescribing essentially architectural matters? What methods could be used to speed public inquiries? The document set out some illustrations of the possible range of developments which would not need permission - for example, house and factory extensions up to one-fifth of the original area instead of one-tenth as before. Those limits might be increased where it was judged possible to relax control, for example, industrial estates, or tightened in specially sensitive areas.

Consultations revealed little unanimity, except on procedural improvements. There was no agreement on the range of developments not needing permission, on the idea of different ranges for different areas, or on new systems for dealing with neighbour problems. Even after a large-scale meeting with all the principal interests it appeared that there was no package of major changes which would command general agreement. One way of looking at this was that the existing planning system held the balance fairly between conflicting interests, so that the lack of agreement did not mean that the review had not been worth while.

In any event, no major changes had been undertaken by the time the Younger administration came to power. The Tories had promised the relaxation of restrictions in general and government controls over local authorities in particular. A good deal was said about the need to release enterprise and cut down central direction, and there seemed to be scope for this in the planning field. The previous proposals for freeing extensions to houses and factories from planning control were revived, but in a proposal which pointed towards closer control the requirements for advertising planning applications were to be widened, so as to give possible objectors a better chance to put their views to the local authority. It was suggested that in order to put the emphasis on development rather than restriction a planning application not decided after two months should be deemed to be granted, not refused, as previously. COSLA gave rather reluctant agreement to thc relaxations of controls over extensions, accepted the principle of advertising more planning applications, but completely rejected the idea of deeming an application to be granted after two months. They thought this would not give local authorities time to consider applications, particularly if more information was needed from the applicant, and that it would lead authorities to issue automatic refusals as the time limit approached.

It was not until nearly two years later, after representations from various sources showed the difficulty of getting unanimous consent to changes in the planning code, that the government decided what to do.[(1)] It might have been thought that given the concern they expressed about restrictions on industry Ministers would have taken the opportunity to decontrol a much wider range of industrial extensions and new construction, but they did not. As regards house extensions, so much concern had been expressed about the effect which extensions might have on amenity that there had to be special arrangements to protect terraces of houses, where uncontrolled extensions might have a particularly severe effect on the appearance of the block and on the enjoyment of other occupiers, and some detailed arrangements to prevent over-development on gardens and other areas within the perimeter. Open-air markets, which had been springing up fast, and had aroused objections from local residents, were to require planning permission. Special types of industrial buildings (generally the more noxious ones) could be used for general industry without seeking permission - an obvious simplification.

The Scottish Office was in two respects more open-handed than the Department of the Environment. The latter kept within planning control any house extension of more than 15% (as against the Scottish 20%) and any industrial extension, however small, within 5 metres of the perimeter of the premises. This degree of control was not felt to be necessary in Scotland, partly because the concern about bad development was less and the desire for industrial development greater. Altogether this was far from being the package of decontrol measures which some would have liked, but in planning, even more than in other areas, one man's meat is another man's poison. Few people tend to welcome uncontrolled development in their own vicinity,

(1) Summarised in SDD Circular No. 24/1981

unless they are doing it themselves, and, in spite of left-wing talk about social control and right-wing talk about setting the people free, views on development control do not follow party lines, and organs of public opinion are equally ambiguous.

In one respect the rules introduced in 1981 made it easier to object to development. Under the building control regulations it had always been necessary to notify neighbours and allow them to put in their objections, but since the granting or refusal of building warrant depended on whether the building met the requirements of the building regulations, and not on planning or other environmental considerations such as neighbours are likely to be interested in, the majority of objections had to be ruled out of order. By that time planning permission had probably already been given. In 1981 the Scottish Office took the logical step of making it necessary to notify neighbours of a planning application rather than of an application for a building warrant. This meant that planning committees would see objections in time to take them into account. At the same time the Scottish Office adjured planning authorities to deal with applications quickly, particularly industrial proposals, while observing approvingly that more than 90% of planning applications are decided within three months.

THE MAKING OF PLANS

The completion of regional structure plans, and still more of local plans, does not usually involve national policies to any great extent; equally it does not produce much public debate on a national scale or statements of national party policy. Furthermore, the procedure for deciding policy in relation to plans is highly formalised by statute and judicial precedents; as with planning applications, once a plan is submitted, the Secretary of State is not open to any further representations by individuals, pressure groups, MPs, or local authorities except through evidence submitted to the public examination or inquiry held on the plan. The policies which the Secretary of State takes account must be stated in his decision, and altogether there is little room for speculation as to how the decision is reached.

INVESTMENT IN THE ENVIRONMENT

County and burgh councils in Scotland had in general been very slow in their preparation of the old style development plans, and the introduction of the new system of two-tier plans, structure and local, more or less coincided with the creation of two-tier local authorities, regions and districts. As we have noted, the regional councils were asked to make their first priority the writing of regional reports, and they responded to this with some enthusiasm. District councils were not precluded from making local plans in the absence of structure plans - in fact planning legislation was specially amended to permit this - but they were considerably inhibited from getting on with them, considering that structure plans were needed to set the main principles of regional development.

After the regional reports were out, the regional planning staffs in most areas made good progress with compiling structure plans. The first to come up for central government approval, that for Orkney, in 1979, presented the Scottish Office with a problem. Opinion in Orkney had been aroused by the news that there might be uranium-bearing ores in the islands, and still more by the application for exploratory drilling submitted by the electricity boards, who saw this as an opportunity for reducing dependence on imported uranium for nuclear power stations. The Orkney community was incensed at the possibility of mining, which they saw as despoiling and endangering their countryside, and ruining their tourist industry, and highly colourful estimates of the degree of radio-activity in mining wastes were current. The electricity boards said their interest in mining was 'fairly long-term', but the regional council sought to conclude the issue once and for all by seeking power to control all prospecting for uranium, and when they lost on this they included a statement in the structure plan that mining for uranium would never be permitted.

This was an extraordinary attempt to determine the future, but it was overwhelmingly supported by the people of Orkney and by many others elsewhere. The Scottish Office was in something of a dilemma. The government, which was committed, with TUC support, to a continued programme of nuclear power, did not accept that uranium mining produced a radioactive hazard, and could not accept a permanent ban on prospecting or mining on purely environmental grounds without regard to the circumstances of each case. Nevertheless it did not want to antagonise Orkney, particularly as the electricity boards' interest in prospecting in Orkney began to wane. Acceptance of the precise wording of the structure plan was out of the question, but excising the statement that prospecting and mining would not be allowed would carry the implication that the government expected it to take place.

George Younger's solution was to reserve judgment on the relevant part of the plan, and to add that the electricity boards had withdrawn their application, and did not now see the need to renew it. If it were renewed, it would be considered in the light of the circumstances of the time. Opinion in Orkney had won a victory for the moment, and although it had not, by this one battle, secured for ever the freedom of the islands from uranium mining, it had served notice that any future attempt would meet the severest resistance. The Secretary of State, for his part, had kept his and his successors' options open.

The Lothian structure plan, which was reaching completion during this time, also involved only one issue of national policy, although a very different one. The Reporter who conducted the Examination in Public of the plan (a public inquiry into a number of issues selected by the Scottish Office, rather than an inquiry into all objections) had recommended that not enough land might have been zoned for housing in the region. George Younger was particularly concerned to get enough land for private housing, and accordingly stipulated that the housing policies should not be effective beyond June 1981 (that is, less than two years instead of the usual five), and that the region should prepare alternative proposals in the meantime, especially for private housing. The other issues in the Lothian plan, although of importance for the region, involved no national policy issues to any great extent.

The same issue of land for private housing was taken up by George Younger on the Strathclyde structure plan. Although the Scottish Office accepted the general policy of infilling or redeveloping existing areas, it insisted that those might not be adequate, especially for private housing. New proposals were called for by the end of 1981, and the general policy that houses should not be built on green field sites was modified for sites of less than half a hectare, so that it would be left to district councils to decide whether to approve them. The limits on private housing targets specified by the regional council were deleted as unrealistic. A more favourable policy towards new town housing was inserted, as was additional land for industry at East Kilbride. On other issues, the Scottish Office deleted the reservation of land for a large natural gas liquids plant, which had been opposed on environmental grounds. Two major road proposals in Glasgow, the Crow Road Expressway and the eastern link, which would have completed the inner ring road, were deleted for similar reasons. The attempt by the regional council to state that new development in the most scenic areas of Strathclyde would be against the regonal strategy was rejected, and decisions on whether to allow development were left to the district councils.

By September 1982, structure plans had been approved by the Secretary of State, or submitted to him for approval, for most of Scotland, the main exceptions being parts of Grampian, Central and Fife regions, and the Western Isles. In most areas local plans had made much less satisfactory progress, even allowing for the difficulty in finalising them while the structure plan was still under consideration. Only about 90 out of over 300 had been adopted, though another 60 had been sent to the regional councils for approval. (Nearly 30 of the adopted plans were in the Highland region, where the regional council is responsible for both types of plan.) These relatively large numbers reveal one of the reasons for poor progress - the decision of district councils to split their areas into a large number of local plan areas (about 50 in Glasgow and 15 in Edinburgh, for example, and five or more in the average district) and to treat them in considerable detail. The Scottish Office, however, did not intervene to secure faster completion, which it regarded as a matter between districts and regions, and there was little public interest in the progress of most of the plans, illustrating once again that general planning policies excite little discussion. It takes a particular case for passions to be aroused.

MOSS MORRAN: POLICY-MAKING IN PUBLIC

There is another means, apart from approving structure plans and making planning guidelines, regulations, or orders, whereby the central government determines policy in planning matters. This is the power of the Secretary of State to call in from the local planning authority any application submitted to it and take over the decision. The national planning guidelines, as we have seen, are in some cases given force by this method, but the call-in procedure is not limited to categories of planning applications where the Scottish Office has announced in advance that it will take over the consideration of the case, and applications are called in wherever it is thought that issues of national importance are at stake. The treatment by the Scottish Office of the application for petrochemical development at Moss Morran and Braefoot Bay is an important example of this, and illustrates other aspects of national planning as well, such as the degree to which environmental and, above all, safety factors are given weight as against economic policy, the extent to which objectors to development can challenge in the courts the decisions of the government, and the effect of new evidence coming to light after a government decision in principle has been made.

Early in 1977 Shell and Esso, after giving up their plans for petrochemical development in the Peterhead area, sought outline planning permission for a natural gas liquids separation plant at Moss Morran in Fife (to be supplied by pipeline from north-east Scotland) together with an ethane cracker, with a shipment jetty at Braefoot Bay, between Aberdour and the new community at Dalgety Bay. An area at Moss Morran was also requested for industrial development, namely manufacturing plant based on the ethylene produced by the ethane cracker. These proposals were the outcome of an extensive search by the companies for sites which might fulfil their requirements in the Cromarty Firth, Teesside, and elsewhere in Fife. The government wanted to promote petrochemical industry in the central belt of Scotland, and West Fife had already been designated as a preferred development area under the national planning guidelines.

INVESTMENT IN THE ENVIRONMENT

Whatever the economical and social factors, however, it has long been established that planning Ministers must act in a quasi-judicial manner when deciding applications or appeals, and must not prejudge their decisions by their statements or actions. Bruce Millan felt that the Moss Morran proposal raised issues of national importance which justified his calling it in for his decision, and promptly did so. The immediate result was to make it impossible for him to speak about the economic importance and indeed any other aspect of the project, in the face of protests from Aberdour and Dalgety Bay, whose inhabitants felt they had nothing to gain from it and much to lose, who obtained more publicity than the economic considerations.

Another result of a government call-in is that a public local inquiry is generally granted if the local authority or the developer ask for it and one is often held if there are strong objections from third parties, whereas a local authority is under less pressure. In retrospect it can be seen that the public inquiry procedure was completed within what must be regarded as a short time for a complex and contentious project. The inquiry finished at the end of July 1977, the reporter compiled an extensive report on it during the rest of the year and decided on his recommendations to the Secretary of State, and by March 1978 Bruce Millan was ready to make a decision. Or rather he would have been, but for one new matter which had emerged since the inquiry was held. This was the possibility that radio transmissions might under certain circumstances cause sparks which might ignite any leak of inflammable gas occurring at a petrochemical plant. New assessments by scientists of the likelihood of this had led in 1977 to the government having to stop radio transmissions from the naval station at Crimond in Aberdeenshire until the possible effect on the nearby St Fergus gas installation had been determined. Bruce Millan regarded the implications for Moss Morran very seriously, and took steps to have them examined.

The Health and Safety Executive had recommended that planning permission should be granted subject to a condition requiring the removal of any source of energy which could cause an ignition hazard, such as a nearby IBA transmitter. It was quite practicable to frame a condition for this purpose, just as it was possible to frame numerous other conditions relating to the capacity and layout of the plant, highways and access, visual impact, drainage arrangements, water, air and noise pollution, and measures against possible safety hazards. Bruce Millan had satisfied himself that, given those conditions, the plants could be designed to operate at an acceptable level of hazard, and that there was an overriding case of need to allow the use of Braefoot Bay in spite of amenity objections.

Why then did he not grant planning permission there and then? The answer lies in the long established rule that Ministerial decisions following an inquiry must not take into account, without giving a further opportunity for comment, matters which arise after the inquiry, or the courts may rule the decision invalid. Either the inquiry must be reopened, or all parties must be given a full opportunity to comment on the new matter. Bruce Millan was anxious to minimise the delay, because the developers and the local authorities (who supported the project) wanted the earliest possible indication that but for this one question of the effect of radio transmissions the green light could be given to the project. He therefore took the unusual course of issuing a lengthy provisional approval, subject to all the conditions suggested and invited representations within 28 days on the condition relating to the means of dealing with possible radio hazards.

It was to be a good deal longer than 28 days before the issue was settled. In the first place, in the light of comments made on the provisional decision letter, the Health and Safety Executive were asked to report in detail on the nature of the radio hazard, and the way of dealing with it. This took several months. Not only that, but their report constituted new evidence, which had to be presented to the objectors with an opportunity for them to comment on it. Further problems arose: the HSE, it emerged, had based their report partly on information supplied by a consultant engaged by Shell, one of the main parties in the case, and the objectors immediately argued that this detracted from the objectivity of the report. They asked to see the Shell consultants' evidence, and when this was refused they applied to the Court of Session, which very pointedly stated that if the Secretary of State continued to refuse to allow the evidence to be made available there was a very real danger of having his decision overturned later. It was, not surprisingly, made available. Then the HSE report was found to contain a number of statements which were technically dubious and they were asked to revise or supplement it. When the supplementary report was received it too had to be sent to the objectors for their comments. The objectors applied to the Court of Session for more time to consider the matter, and the Court indicated that if more time were not given the Secretary of State's eventual decision might be overturned on the grounds that it had been taken without adequate regard to the principles of natural justice.

Meanwhile the objectors took every opportunity to get others to share their concern about the dangers of explosions from causes other than radio sparks; they used evidence from the General Accounting Office of the USA (an independent watchdog agency within the federal machine) to claim that there was danger of an explosion leading to a fireball of burning gas which could reach even across the Forth. This and much other publicity which the objectors obtained for their views was not matched by any similar campaign by Shell-Esso to maintain public support for the project, because they felt that the decision was in the hands of the Secretary of State. Anyone forming an opinion just from what was said in the Press at this time would have come to the conclusion that the dangers of an appalling explosion were so great as to make it inconceivable to carry on the project. The Scottish Office consistently refused however to accept that the question of the danger from the 'conventional' sources should be reopened; that, they said, had been fully canvassed at the inquiry. But the radio question alone was taking months to decide, with every contribution to the debate being laboriously circulated to all the parties represented at the inquiry, and time given to consider it. Even after 12 months it was not possible to make a decision, and Bruce Millan, to his disappointment, was unable to bring the matter to an end before he had to hand over to George Younger.

Naturally the new administration needed time to consider the matter, and it was not until August 1979, that George Younger declared himself satisfied that the plant could be made to operate within an acceptable hazard level, and finally granted planning permission. That was still not the end of the story: the objectors, as was their right, applied to the Court of Session to overturn the decision on the grounds that it had not been properly taken within the Secretary of State's statutory powers. This application was heard at the end of January 1980, and not until the middle of February did the Court make the pronouncement which made it possible for the long-awaited development to start. The Court found the objectors' arguments without the slightest substance, and went so far as to make them pay the defenders' costs. The Court was not of course pronouncing on the merits of the objectors' case on safety or amenity grounds, or whether they were right to pursue their opposition to the project, but merely on their claim that the Scottish Office had not observed the law - including the concept of natural justice - in the way in which it reached a decision. But in any event the Court's finding meant that the objectors, who had won several of the battles in the campaign, had lost the war.

From the point of view of policy analysis, Moss Morran and Braefoot Bay illustrate the principle that the maker of planning policy - the Secretary of State - must not finalise his policy until he is about to reach his decision. Whatever the economic or other benefits of a major development project, he must keep his mind open to all proposals and ensure that every representation, report, or communication which he might take into account is made available for the counter-comments of every other party to the inquiry; and if this is not done at the public hearing it must be done laboriously by correspondence, and by fully circulated correspondence alone, subsequently. The courts will otherwise invalidate the decision. Conversely, the courts will not challenge the decision if it has been reached by the correct procedure. In the light of this there was undoubtedly a considerable risk (from the point of view of the developers) in the provisional decision issued in March 1978, and although it did not in the end invalidate the final decision, the reopening of the inquiry to take into account the question of radio transmissions might have produced less risk and less delays than the exchange of evidence in writing. The need for the Scottish Office's procedure with correspondence to be impeccable allowed the objectors to use their financial and scientific resources (which were very exiguous in comparison with the unlimited resources of the government and the developers) to very good effect in delaying the decision, though they could not stop it in the end.

There is one wryly amusing postscript to this story. Permission for the pipeline from north-east Scotland, on which Moss Morran will be totally dependent, was not finally granted by the Department of Energy until early 1982, two years after the construction of the huge plant had started.

MULLWHARCHAR: RESEARCH INTO THE DISPOSAL OF NUCLEAR WASTE

Governments can take over a planning application, as at Moss Morran; they can also be compelled to do so somewhat against their will as a result of an appeal against a refusal of permission issued by a local planning authority. This is what happened when the UK Atomic Energy Authority applied for permission to sink test boreholes at Mullwharchar, near Loch Doon in Ayrshire. The case is also interesting because it shows a government stating its policy before a planning application was submitted, and disposing of the application by changing policy. In the meantime very strong feelings were aroused, which involved considerations of nuclear power and nuclear weapons which went well beyond the matters with which the application dealt.

Although high-level waste from nuclear power stations had been stored above ground ever since the stations came into production, the possibility of disposing of it by some other means began to be considered as a public issue a good deal later. Disposal in this sense means disposed in some place where it could be allowed to decay over very long periods without further attention, as distinct from storage on a site and in conditions which would be under constant control. The object of the scientists concerned was to undertake research into various rock formations to discover if they would be likely to be suitable for safe disposal, while other research proceeded on converting nuclear waste into a physically stable condition, probably by turning the liquid into a glass-like substance.

By 1977 there was intense discussion of this in Scotland, in the daily press (both 'popular' and 'quality') as well as in technical journals, especially as it became known that two of the rock formations involved in the research programme were in Scotland, in Caithness and at Loch Doon. The planning machinery was involved because the UKAEA needed planning permission to undertake drilling, as this involved 'development' of small parcels of land, even if only for research purposes. Since this minor disturbance of the ground was technically all that was at issue, the government refused to recognise it as a national planning issue by calling in the application. Bruce Millan said in February 1977 that it was for the local authority to give or refuse planning permission, and that he would intervene only if absolutely necessary.

In May, the formal responsibility for policy on the management of nuclear waste was transferred from the Department of Energy to the environmental Ministers - the Secretaries of State for Scotland and Wales and the Secretary of State for the Environment. This emphasised that the question of waste management, whatever form it took, would not simply be regarded as the last stage in nuclear power generation, but as an environmental issue of the greatest importance. It still did not follow, in the government's view, that the borehole applications should be treated as a major planning issue. Thus, for example, the Prime Minister turned down a proposal by George Younger, then in opposition, that the planning applications, which had not yet been submitted, should be suspended.

The objectors refused, however, to accept the government's line that as the boreholes were only for research they carried no wider implications. Existing pressure groups, newly formed groups, and most of the Press publicity, invariably spoke of the borehole applications as a plan to dump deadly waste, and emotive phrases like 'Scotland the nuclear dustbin of Europe' were common. (Not that emotive phrases were entirely the prerogative of one side in the debate: Sir Brian Flowers said at the Royal Institution that the fact that not a single test bore had been drilled was 'almost entirely the fault of the econuts').

When the planning application for the Loch Doon site was submitted in January 1978 the local authorities competed for the right to consider it, as the government still refused to call it in: Strathclyde region tried to take it over from Kyle and Carrick district, the district appealed, and Bruce Millan upheld their appeal. In August they held special open meetings to help them towards making a decision: the chairman asked for speeches to be confined to the question of test-bores, but the opponents of the UKAEA said that it was impossible to deal with the matter without reference to the role of nuclear power. In spite of the UKAEA's repeated claim that the test bores had no direct connection with dumping waste, the district council refused the application in October 1978.

It was obvious that the UKAEA would have to appeal against this decision: they were committed to their programme of research and the chairman of the Radioactive Waste Management Advisory Committee, set up in May 1978, had said that the committee would be unable to give worthwhile advice without sufficient data from research, such as the boreholes. The Labour Government remained equally committed to the programme, and claimed that the transfer of responsibility to the environment Ministers showed that their approach to the problem was socially responsible, and in this they were supported by eminent watchdogs such as the National Radiological Protection Board. But, as in all planning issues, the duty of the Secretary of State to act in an unprejudiced and quasi-judicial manner whenever an appeal to him was imminent silenced the government, while the objectors were under no such limitation, and continued to seek as much publicity as they could - with considerable success, because strong views and colourful statements make good news material.

Moreover some papers clearly saw themselves as conducting a campaign against 'dumping' rather than reporting events. Local opinion in Ayrshire against the Loch Doon application (in contrast with the application in Caithness, where a community accustomed to advanced nuclear enterprises had ensured that the boreholes there were approved without trouble) was so strong that it had political consequences which were in the end to dominate policy. Throughout 1978 George Younger was saying that there was "no great urgency to get rid of nuclear waste in this ham-handed way", and that he was unhappy about the whole principle of burying nuclear waste. The submission of the UKAEA's appeal against the refusal of permission for the Loch Doon boreholes in April 1979, the victory of the Conservatives in the May Election, and the appointment of George Younger as Secretary of State meant that the issue was going to be decided by somebody who had already expressed his views. Naturally the opponents of the scheme did not object to this; the UKAEA could not afford to alienate the government by doing so, and unlike Moss Morran the 'natural justice' argument was conspicuously absent.

The government's official attitude towards the research programme did not however change with the election. It was announced that the local inquiry into the appeal would deal only with the effect of boreholes on the environment, not the wider issues of nuclear policy. Moreover, in July 1979, Michael Heseltine set out a comprehensive statement of the new government's policy which put it even more explicitly behind the programme of research into nuclear waste disposal than anything which had been said previously. The borehole programme was merely research into whether disposal into geological formations was feasible; there was no commitment to disposal on land as against the ocean bed; a wide range of rock types would be researched, and only after about ten years would further research be conducted on two or three sites using actual radioactive waste; and actual disposal of nuclear waste would not be required until the next century. In the meantime the borehole appeals - there were also two in Northumberland - would be decided 'on their merits'. (In view of what happened later, it is interesting that this policy statement was entirely about 'disposal' of nuclear wastes; not a word was said about possible alternatives, such as continued storage above ground).

Preparation for the appeal inquiries went ahead. It was announced that the result of the Loch Doon inquiry reporter would be confined to the environmental effect of the drilling operations only, and in December it was specifically stated that 'to determine the appeal, the Secretary of State is not required to form a view about the desirability of depositing radioactive waste'. Nevertheless, the formal statement of the Secretary of State's position issued in January 1980 before the inquiry opened put the appeal into the context of the programme of waste research necessitated by the nuclear power programme, and the greater part of the lengthy nquiry in February was devoted to the objectors' views on nuclear power and the dangers of the disposal of waste, although the reporter could not deal with those issues in making his recommendations.

INVESTMENT IN THE ENVIRONMENT

Decisions on government planning inquiries are apt to take a long time, but this took longer than most. George Younger, having previously expressed himself as opposed to the test drilling, was now required as Secretary of State to consider the matter impartially. The government was committed to a programme of research the benefits of which would only appear in 10 or 20 years' time, but he was being asked by the UKAEA to make a very unpopular decision now (unpopular at least in the sense that opponents of a planning application are always much more vocal than its supporters).

The inquiry into the last of the UKAEA's applications, in Northumberland, was held at the end of 1980, but the government remained silent throughout 1981. The first indication of what might happen was when the chairman of the UKAEA began to say that "the best way forward for geological disposal will be to continue to cool the blocks (of solidified waste) near the surface until the heat has fallen to a level at which disposal can be recommended", which might be for 50-100 years and more. Why on earth, George Younger may be imagined as saying, did he not say that before putting me through all this agony? And it would be a fair question, since all the scientific facts about the rate of radioactive decay were as well known in 1978 as in 1981. At any rate the way was opened for a reassessment of government policy, and late in December the results were announced. The geological research programme was 'reorientated' to study foreign research on underground disposal; the waste management advisory committee had recommended controlled storage above ground for 50 years or more, and the exploratory drilling applications could therefore be turned down as premature.

Political and public opinion had thus formed a reappraisal of the scientific and technical aspects of nuclear waste management. The community at large had indicated that it could not tolerate the idea of burying waste while it was still highly radioactive, and that another scientifically acceptable solution must be found. The change of policy did not represent politicians overturning proper scientific decisions. It was, however, an important vindication of the right of the community to exercise, through the political process, its right to make the final decision on a matter of public importance.

SCOTLAND'S SCENIC HERITAGE

The protection of the countryside had always been an important motive in planning, especially in its early days. Scotland however had never followed England and Wales in the creation of national parks as a means of conservation and protection, partly because so much of Scotland might qualify and partly because of the resistance of the local authorities to the appointment of special boards which would take over planning functions in the park areas.

This is the essential characteristic of a national park in Britain, where there is no possibility of keeping some areas in an entirely natural state and the most that can be done is to apply special standards of development control. In England and Wales, despite the opposition of local authorities, there was a strong current of public opinion in favour of special protection for the national park areas, to be exercised by bodies with national as well as local representatives on them. In Scotland concern was not so concentrated on a few areas of special importance, and there seemed to be less danger of over-development, with the result that Scottish Ministers were never willing to overrule the objections of the local authorities to the idea of national parks.

There remained one curious vestige of the 1940s, when it was thought that national parks might be created in Scotland. These were five 'National Park Direction Areas', which were intended to be the precursors of national parks, but remained for thirty years in embryo form, as areas in which all development proposals had to be notified to the Scottish Office to enable the latter to decide whether to call them in or not. It is remarkable that this degree of central control persisted, without much friction, long after there was any real likelihood of national parks being created in Scotland.

The creation of the Countryside Commission for Scotland in 1965 was in a sense a conclusive move away from the national park philosophy, since the Commission was empowered to provide guidance and financial assistance to any non-urban area: the whole of the Scottish countryside was a heritage to be cared for. (At a later date this philosophy was applied in England and Wales, but the national parks were retained.)

In course of time, however, the Commission sought to revive the idea of national parks - properly renamed special parks, since the international criteria for national parks as wilderness areas cannot be met in Britain. These would be the top tier in a hierarchy of parks of different kinds, including local country parks and regional parks. In spite of the similarity of name, however, special parks would be of a different species - not areas devoted to recreation, but areas of scenic conservation and special development control. Bruce Millan's administration, though approving the system in principle, was not willing to take action against the opposition of local authorities, which was as strong as ever. Only in the case of Loch Lomond was there local authority support for anything in the nature of a national park and even here the local authorities, while willing to co-ordinate their policies and anxious to attract central funds, wanted to run the show themselves.

The Commission began to place more weight on an idea also broached in their report 'A Park System for Scotland', namely the identification of the areas of the best scenery in Scotland, more numerous and wider-ranging in character than the old national park designation areas, but in most cases too small by any standards to justify a separate planning authority. In the course of 1976 and 1977 the Commission's staff analysed the majority of the potential areas in Scotland, not by fixed criteria but by taking account of all the characteristics of each area and the factors affecting it, and early in 1978 the Commission published their analysis of 40 areas of first class scenic importance in 'Scotland's Scenic Heritage'. The Scottish Development Department circulated this to all planning authorities, to take it into account in framing their own planning policies, and also suggested to COSLA that it should be used as a basis for a National Planning Guideline on the protection of Scotland's scenery. The guideline philosophy was to draw a distinction between matters of local and matters of national concern, and in this case the 40 areas were to be regarded as of national concern, which meant that SDD would be notified of potentially intrusive development which the local planning authority proposed to allow within them.

If there was to be any central control at all, this system had attractions for local authorities over the national park direction system: the 40 areas were in total less than the areas covered by the directions, and instead of all planning applications being notified to Edinburgh only limited categories would be notified. Discussions between SDD and COSLA in 1978 and 1979 indicated that the latter would approve the system, which crystallised in the form of a requirement on the local authority to consult the Countryside Commission about proposals for 5 or more houses or caravans, developments exceeding half a hectare, buildings over 12 metres high, vehicle tracks above the 300 metres contour and new roads; the Secretary of State would have to be notified if the local authority then proposed to give permission against the advice of the Commission.

These proposals also contained another new policy initiative in that for the first time in Scotland agriculture and forestry would, in the scenic areas, be brought within planning control in respect of tall buildings and vehicle tracks on the hills, both of which were beginning to make a considerable impact on the landscape.

COSLA agreed with the plan, and with minor changes it was given effect from August 1980. Notification of development within the National Park Direction Areas was given up, as was notification of development in the preferred conservation zones in the coastal planning guidelines, so that the new system did not just constitute an extension of central control.

The Highland Regional Council had however bitterly opposed these measures from the start, on the grounds that they were themselves best equipped to decide the national as well as the local interest, that the Countryside Commission was opposed to development and did not understand the need to promote growth and employment in the Highlands, and that it was wrong for an elected authority to be subject to the intervention of a non-elected body. Emotive expressions were used such as the need to have a living countryside, not one fossilised in a state of decay according to a city dweller's romantic vision, and the danger of frightening off foreign investors.

These views were not shared by COSLA as a whole, which gave its approval in the knowledge that the Highland Regional Council was opposed. The MPs in the Highlands intervened to support the council, but George Younger replied that they were under "a fairly major misconception", since the Countryside Commission would be only an adviser. Final decisions would rest with him, and it was less than justice to assume that he would allow the system to stifle much needed development. But in response to the objections, which were shared by members of his own party, he decided to delay the operation of the new system in the Highlands (and also in the Western Isles, whose council had also decided to join in) for a year, to allow for preparation and adaptation of the new control procedure, and give an opportunity for it to be seen in operation elsewhere.

At this stage COSLA abruptly changed sides, describing the new system as unnecessary and burdensome, and had to be reminded that the matter had already been settled, on the basis of their previous agreement, by the issue of the necessary regulations. Meanwhile the Highland Council was deciding whether to act on the Secretary of State's suggestion that they should try to establish a way of living with the new system, and after some months they had an exchange of letters with the Commission, which may have helped to clear the air. The regulations had been drafted to come into effect automatically in the Highlands and Western Isles in August 1981, without the need for the issue of a further statutory instrument, and so it came to pass.

As with most planning issues (with the outstanding exception of land values and ownership) national party politics had played no part in determining policy on scenic areas, nor had there been a great deal of public interest outside the Highlands. This was because the Commission's proposals were essentially of a compromise nature, as compared with their earlier advocacy of special part authorities with planning powers. The dispute with the Highland Council was a manifestation of the region's long-standing claim for special treatment appropriate to its distinctive character, not only in planning but in many other fields - a claim which will no doubt continue to be pressed as long as the Highlands exist. On this occasion the claim was not, in the end, accepted; national considerations had prevailed over local, in the sense that some developments in some areas could be referred to the Secretary of State by a centrally appointed body instead of being decided by the local authorities alone.

TOWN AND COUNTRY PLANNING

In the first two years of the scheme, however, the Countryside Commission, out of 60 planning applications about which they were consulted, recommended rejection in only 5 cases (none of which were in the Highlands or Western Isles), and no major disagreements between the Commission and the local authorities had arisen. The Commission had suggested in about two-thirds of the applications that planning permission should be given subject to conditions, which goes a long way to confirming the Commission's claim that the system would not be used to stop development, but to ensure that it fitted in better with the landscape, which in those 40 areas more than anywhere else was part of the national heritage.

CHAPTER IV

TRANSPORT POLICIES

Any discussion of transport policy must face the question of whether there is, or can be, a distinct policy for Scotland or whether it is an aspect of policy for Great Britain as a whole. The question is in fact too simple, because the disparities between the different modes of transport - between road and rail, between private and public transport, and between all these and sea and air transport - are such that a single answer does not make sense except to outright nationalists. But the degree of policy independence, however much it varies, is something to be taken into account in examining the origin of decisions on each of the different aspects of transport.

Formally and constitutionally, the responsibilities of the Secretary of State for Scotland and of the Secretary of State (formerly the Minister) for Transport, are clear. The Secretary of State for Scotland has traditionally looked after sea ferries to the islands, and took responsibility for roads in the 1950s. Much later, in the 1970s, he assumed responsibility for subsidising air services to the islands, and his function of overseeing local authorities embraces their responsibility for subsidising passenger transport services, whether bus or rail, in their areas. Inter-city rail services and the main air services and airports are not formally his concern, but no important initiative would be taken without consulting him. Road safety policy is his, but not licensing and the setting of standards either for drivers or for vehicles - in fact these are the fields of transport policy in which he has the least responsibility except of course as a member of the Cabinet.

TRANSPORT POLICY CONSULTATIONS: THE SCOTTISH INFLUENCE

The role of Scotland in formulating the Labour government's transport policy in the 1970s therefore differed greatly according to subject. In 1976 the government published a consultation document[1] which "represents the outcome of a comprehensive review of transport policy", motivated in general by the increasing public debate on transport questions and in particular by the strength of the rail unions and other railway interests within the Labour party, who expected a Labour government to make a massive switch to investment in rail. It proved to be a more balanced document than this, describing the gain from a road to rail switch as marginal, and stressing our contradictory and conflicting attitudes to transport questions.

Scotland and Wales enjoyed a separate chapter, which began by saying that to a large extent transport in Scotland and Wales forms an integral part of the transport system of Great Britain, and that virtually everything that was said in the earlier parts of the consultation document applied equally to those countries. Nevertheless, it said, the formulation of transport policies must take full account of the special characteristics and different institutions of Scotland and Wales. There must, for example, be a difference in the emphasis of investment programmes in Scotland, because of the need to improve and complete the long-distance road links, between the oil development areas in the north of Scotland and the central industrial belt, and between the central belt and England. The special needs of the sparsely-populated rural areas and the need for support for uneconomic ferry services and air services to the islands must also be taken into account. With the strict limits on public expenditure applying in 1976 this was a clear indication that no single interest could be fully satisfied, and that there would have to be compromise. Public transport services (including concessionary fares) had been exempted from cuts in the 1976 White Paper on Public Expenditure, but even there "the Government would welcome observations on whether the balance suggested in the White Paper seems right".

---

(1) Transport Policy, a Consultation Document. HMSO April 1976

INVESTMENT IN THE ENVIRONMENT

It fell to the Scottish Office to collect those observations from interests and organisations in Scotland, and a lengthy round of correspondence and meetings ensued. This well illustrates the pattern of consultation on policy making on a subject which is of public importance, but not a major inter-party issue.

Comments were received from most of the Regional and Island Councils, and from a minority of District Councils. In the main, local authorities concentrated on local rather than national issues, though they were united in opposing cuts in expenditure either on roads or on public transport. They wanted a greater degree of selectiveness in public transport subsidies but there were few suggestions as to how this might be achieved. There was common ground among the regional authorities on the special transport needs of rural areas, supported by subsidy which discriminates in their favour; an opposition to reductions in road maintenance; on the need to avoid general measures to penalise the private motorist and road freight which would increase costs in rural areas; and on the need for more attention to air and sea transport. A major increase in the powers of local authorities over public transport was advocated by a number of authorities.

Strathclyde, the biggest region and least local in their outlook, accepted limitations on road expenditure, although not on maintenance, and approved of increased restraint of the private car in towns and of increased traffic management. In support of public transport they advocated discriminatory pricing and subsidies to deal with peak travel and to meet social needs.

Among the other regional councils, Grampian placed very strong emphasis on local authorities as the basis for the organisation of transport, and sought greater responsibility for public transport. They showed a general scepticism about long-term planning, road investment assessment techniques, environmental issues or experimentation with unconventional forms of public transport under the licensing system. Like others, they put particular emphasis on road safety as a factor in road design, planning, and maintenance, and in other minor ways.

TRANSPORT POLICIES

Central Region showed a predominant interest in public transport, including local authority representation on the board of the Scottish Transport Group. They wanted greater control of the operation of road passenger transport which is totally within their area, and control over the licensing and operation of non-standard facilities, such as community school buses. In pursuance of discriminatory subsidies they were prepared to see higher bus and rail fares, and they supported differential off-peak fares as a means of reducing the cost of concessionary fares schemes. They argued that a separate roads investment assessment technique which is suitable for Scottish conditions should be developed and that lower traffic flows should not prejudice the acceptance of road schemes in Scotland. (In fact this had long been the case. Scottish policy on roads, which had been set out in 1969 in a White Paper [1] - before English policy had been announced - justified construction on geographical and economic development grounds, with little emphasis on formal cost-benefit analysis.)

In the case of the National Union of Railwaymen, the general line was predictably that road investment had been over-emphasised and that the possibilities of rail had not been appreciated. They opposed buses replacing rail services but advocated more money for buses both from local authorities and via a reduction in roads expenditure. They argued that Scotland has a special dependence on public transport and that rail investment should be increased in order to re-open some Scottish lines and to extend electrification to serve oil development. Rail closures in the meantime, they considered, would pre-empt a future Scottish assembly's decision (though it was unlikely, even in 1976, that an assembly would have any responsibility for main rail routes).

There was a substantial body of comment from industrial and commercial interests in Scotland. The Confederation of British Industry said that the transport needs of industry are paramount because only the increased wealth generated by industry can be used to fund social programmes. A strict financial regime for the nationalised transport industries was advocated, together with less government interference with management decisions. They accepted the idea of an advisory National Transport Council broached in the consultation document, and proposed a separate

(1) Scottish Roads in the 1970s (Cmnd 3953)

Scottish council with corresponding devolved management for the nationalised sectors. Transport problems, they thought, were too urgent to await the attention of an assembly and organisational changes should proceed as soon as possible. They expressed concern about transport in remote areas and advocated greater flexibility in the licensing system particularly in the Highlands and Islands.

The Scottish Council (Development and Industry) similarly proposed a new organisational structure for Scottish transport in advance of devolution, but were not in favour of a National Transport Council. They considered that roads investment had too high a priority and that there was significant scope for the transfer of freight from road to rail, particularly as electricity would be the main source of power at the turn of the century, demanding a fully electrified rail network.

The National Farmers' Union in Scotland submitted a lengthy analysis of the general transport problems of rural areas. Transport subsidy should be area-based, to provide passenger and freight services in rural areas at a reasonable cost, with greater emphasis on buses than rail services. Better planning of bus services and bus-rail co-ordination was sought and road equivalent tariff pricing for ferries was advocated. Subsidies to public transport must however be accompanied by favourable treatment for private motorists in remote rural areas, with reductions in vehicle taxation and rebates on fuel oil taxes. Consistent with this general argument, the NFUS favoured relaxation of bus licensing and opposed EEC regulations for cutting lorry drivers' hours of work.

The views of organisations representing transport operators were not unexpectedly coloured by the mode of transport they represented, and no substantially new arguments were presented. With the exception of the Scottish National Party and the Scottish Liberal Party, there was little comment from political organisations. The SNP favoured, as might be expected, a Scottish transport co-ordinating authority, accountable to the assembly, and responsible for all aspects of policy but not for the operation of transport services. The Consultation Document was criticised for inadequate attention to Scotland, particularly air services and coastal shipping.

TRANSPORT POLICIES

The comments of the Scottish Liberal Party were determined by the party's views on federalism: there should be a UK body for federal co-ordination of transport, but separate ownership of all transport resources under the control of a Scottish Transport Executive, which would be responsible for the licensing and consumer representation as well as the control and operation of transport. Public transport would be encouraged and the urban private car discouraged. Rail freight would be preferred to road freight, partly through better grants for rail sidings. Rural transport would be given priority and experimentation with unconventional forms of public transport encouraged.

The representations of pressure groups reinforced their known views. Transport Action Scotland favoured increased roads investment, set out a priority road programme for Scotland in detail, and argued that increased roads investment should be funded out of reductions in public transport subsidies. They opposed all subsidies with the exception of rural bus subsidies and temporary support for experimental or innovatory public transport. They argued that lorries already bore their full share of resource costs.

The Scottish Association for Public Transport claimed that the Consultation Document failed to recognise the distinctive Scottish aspects of transport problems. They wanted a Scottish Transport Department with overall responsibility for transport in Scotland, prior to devolution, but eventually responsible to a Minister of Transport within the assembly. Their broad lines of transport policy were a severe curtailment of roads investment, particularly the strategic trunk roads network; a large scale shift of public expenditure to public transport, mainly for investment, with subsidies being retained only for specific needs; within public transport a priority for rail over bus transport; measures to ensure that road users are charged to cover the costs they create and a general restraint on the private car including the possibility of direct road pricing by journey length and toll charges; in the freight field preference for rail over road mainly through increased charges and restrictions on road haulage; and greater concern for road safety and the pedestrian.

The Automobile Association, on the other hand, spoke in favour of a large roads programme with priority given to roads linking industrial centres and ports. In general they were opposed to all public transport subsidies and argued that since private transport is available to nearly everyone only public transport which can meet its costs should be retained; the needs of rural areas should be met by unconventional forms of public transport where necessary. They were, of course, critical of any attempt to restrain use of the private car of impose extra costs on the private motorist. They doubted the influence of a National Transport Council and were critical of the representation suggested in the Consultation Document.

At a fairly late stage in the consultations there was a debate in the House of Commons, but as no Scottish member from either side took part it has little relevance to a study of Scottish policy-making. When the government's conclusions appeared, in the form of the White Paper on Transport Policy [(1)], it reiterated that transport in Scotland and Wales forms an integral part of the system for Great Britain and gave an assurance that the comments of Scottish and Welsh interests had been taken into account. Where, in the text of the White Paper, there were significant differences in policy for Scotland or Wales, they were dealt with subject by subject, rather than in a separate chapter, thus emphasising integration rather than the separatist argument.

Special references to Scottish circumstances were made in four areas - the effect of devolution, rural areas and ferry services, the Scottish Bus Group, and the roads programme, reflecting the functions in which the Scottish Office had prime responsibility. The comment on devolution was simply to the effect that the freedom of action in a devolved assembly would not be inhibited by the proposals in the White Paper - a standard assurance common to government pronouncements at that time. The section on rural and remote areas noted the importance of local air services in Scotland and the amount of financial assistance given to them and to the associated airfields. In relation to ferry services it considered and rejected the case for a 'road equivalent tariff',

---

(1) Cmnd 6836

on the ground that the government could not justify doubling the amount of subsidy paid, and because of the objections to dissociating charges from costs. This decision and the reasons given for it - particularly the second - are of interest in view of the Conservative election manifesto two years later, and the course of events under the Conservative administration. The Scottish Bus Group - one of the few nationalised industries under the direct control of the Scottish Office - was applauded for so nearly breaking even over 8 years and reducing its demands on the local authorities for bus subsidies, and no major changes were proposed.

The section of the White Paper on roads illustrates how the Scottish Office typically sets out, in a subject in which it has full responsibility, a policy which is different from that in England. The White Paper recognised, that "different emphases" were necessary in England, Scotland and Wales and then explained at some length the reasons for a substantial reduction of the English road programme, such as concern about the environmental effects of road building, doubts about the amount of new road capacity needed, and the need to restrict public expenditure. Only the last of these was relevant to Scotland: except in the cities, there had been no opposition to roads on environmental grounds, and the public pressure was overwhelmingly for more roads on economic grounds, namely the extent to which it was thought good roads would benefit and attract industry. The Scottish Office was not substantially reducing its road programme, so it relied on the 8-year-old policy set out in 'Scottish Roads in the 1970s' and proposed no fundamental changes in it, although there was a warning about the need for reconsideration of the standards to which roads were constructed.

The Scottish organisations which had studied the original consultation document had made observations on a far wider variety of subjects than those which were given a separate Scottish section in the White Paper. It fell to the Department of Transport rather than the Scottish Office to assess these, because they were 'Great Britain' subjects on which there was no scope for a distinctively Scottish policy. In the main this seemed to be accepted, and few if any of the comments on the White Paper criticised it. Rail policy in particular was, as before, accepted as a matter which must be treated as an all-Britain question, in spite of the intense concern which any rumour or proposal about the closure of a Scottish rail service arouses.

Transport policy accordingly did not play a major part in the devolution debate of the next two years, and the Scottish Office got on with implementing its road programme, although with some delays, and its standstill policy on monetary aid to ferry services to the islands, with little change until 1979.

Early in that year, Bruce Millan modified his policy to the extent of announcing a general subsidy, for the first time, for Orkney and Shetland. The island councils had long pressed for government help, and their success in obtaining a change in policy was aided by the consistent support of their MP, Jo Grimond. It was a strictly limited measure of assistance that was announced - no help for passenger services, and less subsidy for northbound freight traffic than for southbound, in spite of complaints of the cost of conveying goods from the mainland. It emerged that a substantial proportion of goods are conveyed to the islands carriage-paid, which meant that the subsidy on northbound goods would tend to go to the suppliers rather than to the people of the islands. Conversely, a high subsidy on southbound traffic would promote islands produce and manufactures.

THE CONSERVATIVES' POLICIES

The Conservative election manifesto for Scotland in 1979 introduced a new element into the situation. In spite of the general emphasis on the need for reductions in public expenditure, it contained two unusually specific and detailed commitments - which were in fact the only stated policies on Scottish transport in the whole manifesto. One was that the road from Aberdeen to Perth would be reconstructed to "at least the standard of a dual carriageway", and the other was that the Conservatives would increase subsidies to the islands "as part of the process of moving closer to road equivalent tariffs". These commitments deserve special examination, because they illustrate the making of policy by political parties when in Opposition.

The claim that Aberdeen, as the country's main port and centre for the oil industry, should have a dual carriageway to the south had been pressed for a long time, except on the part of governments which would have to pay for the scheme and rate its priority against that of other road schemes. Action was delayed to some extent by a persistent dispute about which was the best road to improve - the coast route, namely the existing trunk road A92, or the inland route A94 through Brechin and Forfar. If a change was to be made, the local authorities wanted as much to be done at government expense on the old trunk road before it was handed over to them. Meanwhile the Scottish Office got on with improvements at government expense, which would not normally have applied until the road was finally trunked in 1978 - but to single carriageway standard only. This paralleled the history of the rebuilding of the A9 to Inverness, where earlier plans to dual the road all the way had not been pursued. In both cases the present and forecast traffic was well below the level which demands a dual carriageway, as against a single carriageway reconstructed throughout to high standards.

The situation was somewhat like that of Edinburgh, where the distribution of traffic between three main roads to the south meant that none of them carries anything like the number of vehicles justifying a motorway. In the case of Aberdeen, however, local pressures and their influence on the Conservative party produced in 1979 the commitment to build a dual carriageway - perhaps even a motorway - notwithstanding the general commitment to reduce public expenditure, and the fact that several sections of the road improved during the preceding few years would have to be rebuilt a second time.

The Scottish Development Department, after the Conservative victory in the election, worked out a programme for fitting the new road into a road programme which in total was no larger than before. The annual policy statement on roads in Scotland for 1980 [1] - a legacy of Labour's

---

(1) Roads in Scotland, 1980. SDD (not HMSO)

White Paper on Transport - promised that the reconstruction of the road would be completed by the late 1980s. Such a new commitment meant putting back other schemes, but the policy statement concentrated on what could still be done, and when.

The programme for Scottish road and passenger subsidy received relatively favoured treatment in the new government's expenditure plans. The programme submitted to the Committee on Scottish Affairs in 1981(1) showed only a 5% decrease between 1980-81 and 1982-83, as compared with 21% for housing. The public expenditure plans of March 1982 and February 1983 forecast an actual increase in transport expenditure in cash terms, and probably also in volume terms. It might be said that this merely showed an animus against public sector housing, but Conservatives would point out in reply that the housing cuts were mainly concerned with current expenditure - more revenue from rents, in fact, and less from rates and subsidies - and that if the housebuilding programme was compared with the roadbuilding programme there was no difference in treatment. In any case roads are a field in which there is little chance of private building offsetting the cuts in the public sector: if roads are to be built, they have so far been built and funded by public authorities. Meanwhile the table on roads and transport expenditure plans suggests that the momentum of the programme is secure for several more years.

THE CONSERVATIVES AND THE ISLANDS

Like the dualling of the Aberdeen road, the proposal for a road equivalent tariff for ferry services to the islands was not new(2) . What was new was the Tory 1979 manifesto commitment to 'move closer' to it, when it had been rejected by the Labour government on two grounds which should have appealed to the Tories - that it would cost more, and that it would mean that charges were not related to costs. Attitudes towards ferry subsidies

---

(1) Committee on Scottish Affairs 15.6.81: Scottish Office Memorandum on Expenditure.

(2) One of the main progenitors of the idea was the Highlands and Islands Development Board: see its report 'Roads to the Isles', December 1974.

ACTUAL AND PLANNED PUBLIC EXPENDITURE ON ROADS AND TRANSPORT IN SCOTLAND (£ million)

White Paper on Public Expenditure	Date	Price basis	Year 1975-76	1976-77	1977-78	1978-79	1979-80	1980-81	1981-82	1982-83	1983-84	1984-85
Cmnd.7049	Jan.78	1977 survey	261	241	257	249	255	258	258			
" 7439	Jan.79	1978 "	295	273	272	280	285	287	287	287		
" 7841	Mar.80	1979 "	320	299	307	325	313	303	300	280	280	
" 8175	Mar.81	1980 "	389	350	372	394	379	355	352	340	340	
" 8494	Mar.82	Cash		234	272	324	372	434	494	499	530	560
" 8789	Feb.83	Cash			272	324	374	434	492	555	524	550

NOTES:

1. Figures to the left of the line are historical: figures to the right are future proposals.

2. The adoption of the cash basis in 1982 makes direct comparison with the White Papers for earlier years impossible, without the application of the price conversion percentages given in section 5.12 of Cmnd.8494.

3. The February 1983 White Paper assumes 5% inflation between 1982-83 and 1983-84. This must be taken into account in considering the likely value, in purchasing power, of the expenditure for the two years.

seem to depend less, however, on political allegiance than on appeal to particular local interests. In opposition, moreover, a party takes a much more generous view of what the government can do than when it forms the government itself.

The Tory manifesto commitment did allow some room for manoeuvre, in that it was not an explicit commitment to road equivalent tariffs, but an undertaking to increase ferry subsidies in real terms, so as to approach the RET system. The consultative paper by the Scottish Development Department (1) which George Younger authorised presented a different picture from that which the islanders might have expected, and contained reservations not forecast in the manifesto. It conceded that RET "does remain a policy option", but the emphasis was heavily on two other possibilities.

First, however, it was necessary to define RET. Although some hoped it meant a charge per mile of a ferry crossing equivalent only to the running costs of a vehicle for a mile (fuel, oil and maintenance) SDD agreed that it must also include standing charges such as drivers' wages, insurance, and licensing, because those are charges which would have to be apportioned over the mileage travelled even if the journey were by road. There would also be an element of toll "designed to produce a reasonable minimum fare even on the shortest crossings". (The charge for crossing to Skye from Kyle of Lochalsh, for example, would otherwise hardly be worth collecting.)

Applying this system, SDD said that it would certainly make freight traffic cheaper, especially to the nearer islands, but cars would pay more to the more distant islands, including Shetland, because the current long-distance rates were very favourable. But fixing ferry charges by reference to road costs and not to costs actually incurred would create extra demand irrespective of costs, especially in the peak tourist season. The ferry operators would have a guarantee of subsidy to make up any deficit, and however good their motivation the absence of financial discipline would seriously undermine incentives to efficiency. As a result, the government would find itself making the decisions on the nature and frequency of the services.

---

(1) 'Sea Transport to the Scottish Islands' SDD, March 1980 (not HMSO)

In consequence two further options were considered - to use RET as a guide to the amount of subsidy to be offered, but taking into account public expenditure plans and the scope for economy and efficiency in the services; and RET applied to freight traffic only, which would not create a new summer peak and would preserve the ferry operators' incentives to efficiency on their passenger and car services. The government also said that it was considering offering subsidy to additional operators, and putting the right to operate certain services out to tender, in spite of considerable difficulties in getting fixed bids or persuading potential operators to make bids at all without a guarantee of a long contract.

The consultative document ended by inviting comments and nearly 70 organisations responded to this, with observations varying from those of around 30 organisations which simply asked for RET to be adopted, to the lengthy and carefully considered observations of the Western Isles Council (which commissioned consultants to report on the matter, and changed its views in so doing), the Highlands and Islands Development Board, the Scottish Transport Group, and P & O Ferries. Most of the points in the consultative paper attracted comment, except the suggestion that RET rates could be used as a guide to subsidy; this was too pragmatic a proposal to recommend itself to those who favoured a simple and apparently straightforward principle such as RET although it would not have been difficult to foresee that it would prove more attractive to the government in the long run than any fixed principle of operation.

Fifty or more organisations supported the principle of RET, although nearly all were islands areas, district or community councils, and local island industries who were clearly anxious to accept any potential reduction in the ferry charges.

A dozen or so major organisations opposed the introduction of RET. These included Strathclyde Regional Council, the Western Islands Council, Shetland Islands Council, the Scottish Transport Group and P & O. Some of these thought that RET would give little benefit to the islands (most of the support would "leak" elsewhere): direct assistance to island economies would be preferable. Others thought that RET was an inequitable and unreasonable way to distribute ferry support. They thought that a tapering charge for distance - related to ferry costs - was preferable. Others again (including the ferry operators and academic commentators) saw the real benefit to the islands coming from ensuring efficient operation of the ferry system. There was however surprisingly little comment on the observation in the consultative paper that RET would militate against efficiency by providing subsidy irrespective of costs.

As to the method of calculation of RET, the HIDB proposed the calculation of RET on the running costs of a vehicle. This had the effect of reducing fares very much further than the operating cost level proposed in the consultative paper, and was favoured by most RET supporters. Of those who commented on the proposal that RET should be applied to freight traffic only, the majority were against it. Those opposed to freight-only RET argued that tourism was important to the islands and that it would be encouraged by reduced car fares. On the other hand those in favour of freight-only RET saw it as a means of making assistance a little more selective.

There was a good deal of support for awarding route licences on a competitive basis. Those who opposed the suggestion were generally islands interests, particularly smaller communities who argued that route licensing would deprive them of a guaranteed service. Other respondents emphasised the practical difficulties: for example, existing operators owned terminal facilities, the capital costs of bidding for a licence would be prohibitive, there were no alternative operators. Those in favour of the proposal saw it as a means of inculcating efficiency or as a means of stimulating competition both of which should reduce costs. There were also a number of respondents who thought that any proposal which offered an alternative operator to the present one would produce a more luxurious, frequent and cheaper service.

Thirteen bodies, mainly islands interests, commented on the importance of providing support for bulk cargo services. Scottish Transport Group suggested that bulk shipping should be replaced by roll-on/roll-off services for all but a very few specialised cargoes. Six organisations proposed discounts for regular travellers in addition to RET. It was argued that this would maintain additional benefit for local traffic over tourist traffic during the summer season. A number of respondents also argued for specific subsidies in addition to RET to be given principally for agricultural inputs. Several saw discount schemes and specific subsidies as a more flexible and selective form of assistance than RET itself.

The local authorities argued that if RET were introduced it should be applied equally to services subsidised by central and local government, by means of additional central government subsidy. HIDB and others recognised that the routes, vessels and terminals used would have to be reconsidered if RET were introduced, in order to reduce costs.

Neither the Scottish Transport Group nor P & O were in favour of the proposals, which could be seen to threaten their existing near-monopolies. However, they both produced lengthy responses which discussed a number of practical and commercial difficulties with RET and route licensing, and the Scottish Transport Group produced a useful account of an alternative charging system. There were no responses from potential operators under a route licensing system.

As with many consultative exercises, the responses were largely predictable, as most of the commentators looked at the problem from the point of view of their limited interest. This characterises the difference between organisations outside government, which have no responsibility outside the areas or interests they represent, and government itself, which must make the best attempt it can to take account of the overall consequences of any policy it adopts and of the interests of all sections of the community. This is obviously restricted by a manifesto commitment, but cannot be ignored entirely by a government with the responsibilities of office.

The mixed response on RET was succeeded by a long period of silence from the Scottish Office. Eventually, in July 1981, there was a Parliamentary written statement which noted that not everybody favoured RET, that Norway (whose example had often been quoted) did not operate RET, that RET would have to be modified so as to help the longer routes, and that the aim was "to introduce a system from 1982/83 leading towards an RET basis". In addition, it was forecast, there would be some 'restructuring' of the subsidy system, to enable support given to particular ferry services to be more clearly identifiable than in the past.

The first experiment in such restructuring did not prove a very happy or successful one. For some years, two services, one nationalised, the other private, had been competing on the routes between Dunoon and the eastern side of the Clyde estuary. In July 1981 the Scottish Office announced that the subsidy to the nationalised Caledonian MacBrayne would be ended; instead, Western Ferries, who for a long time had been complaining about subsidies to the nationalised undertaking on both the Clyde and the Islay routes, would be given a capital grant for a new ferry on the Clyde in return for putting on a high-speed passenger service with the aid of a one-year subsidy. This was treated as a politically-motivated decision by Labour MPs and Strathclyde Regional Council, but it also met more general opposition from Dunoon interests, as the ferry terminal would not be in Dunoon but a mile or so away.

A change in the government's plan came in the autumn, when Western Ferries' high speed passenger plan was dropped and Cal/Mac agreed to carry on at least their passenger service. Then in February 1982 it was announced that Cal/Mac would continue to be subsidised on this service after all. In the light of evidence not previously available, it was said the original plan was found to be unrealistic. However, the government claimed that they had achieved their object of reducing subsidies. Meanwhile Western Ferries' Islay service, the only other real contender under any system for granting route licences on a competitive basis, had gone out of business, with bitter complaints about government subsidy to Cal/Mac, and counter-claims that Western Ferries could not provide a guaranteed all-year-round service.

In March 1982, Malcolm Rifkind explained to the House of Commons Committee on Scottish Affairs the government's latest thinking on RET. After observing that most of those consulted simply wanted financial support to be increased irrespective of method and quoting the administration's record in doubling financial support (in money rather than real terms) in three years, he said that the aim was to introduce a fare structure consistent with moving towards RET in 1983/84 (no longer 1982/83). The government would make an assessment of what the subsidy would be for each route under RET, and then decide what resources it could afford to distribute on this basis. This was virtually the system of using

RET as a guide to subsidy which had not attracted many of those consulted, and was about the only way in which George Younger's administration could avoid an open-ended subsidy without being accused of going back on its manifesto commitment. Money for the full application of RET was not available, so that the problem of how to operate RET while maintaining limits on public expenditure and preserving incentives to economy and efficiency was still unsolved.

Meanwhile MPs were examining the matter in another forum, namely the Committee on Scottish Affairs, which heard evidence throughout the early months of 1982, and issued a report on 19 May.(1) Like earlier reports of the Committee, it provided a convenient and authoritative summary of the current situation and how it had arisen, which, in the case of ferry subsidies, had not been the result of a preconceived policy applied equally to different routes, but of 'help being applied in each particular situation in the way that seemed best at the time'. Thus in the case of the Caledonian MacBrayne services on the west coast and Hebrides, annual negotiations with the Scottish Office led to the establishment of a financial target as with other nationalised industries (in this case, break-even after payment of subsidy). The more recent subsidy for services to and from Orkney and Shetland, as mentioned earlier, is on the basis of rebating the tariffs charged by P & O Ferries Ltd., while the internal Orkney services simply have their deficits met by central government.

Like most committees examining a problem as outsiders (or with fresh minds, as others might say) the Scottish Committee was attracted by the concept of a uniform and comprehensive policy, in this instance a long-term strategy based on road equivalent tariff. Although it was conceded that there were some objections to RET, such as the view of P & O that the application of road transport economics to the realities of ship operation was completely impractical, the Committee found an "overwhelming groundswell of opinion in favour of the early and general introduction of RET", and asked the government to commit themselves to full RET in 1984/85.

---

(1) Second report from Committee on Scottish Affairs 1981-82 'Rural Road Passenger Transport and Ferries'

It was, however, easier for the Committee to urge extra expenditure than for the government, whatever their manifesto commitment, to agree to it. George Younger's response(1) claimed credit for the increases in subsidies which he had introduced, but described the Committee's recommendation, which would require a doubling of support, as unrealistic. (This, it will be remembered, is precisely what the Labour government had said five years earlier.) Although the government accepted a number of the Committee's other recommendations, it is clear that on the issue of road equivalent tariff the findings of a group of MPs are not going to deflect it from the policy which it has in practice had to adopt since taking office. Only time will show whether the report and the "groundswell of opinion" will result in a final commitment to road equivalent tariff, but there is little doubt that if it occurs it will come through a Party decision and not through parliamentary committees. Up to 1983, in any event, George Younger continued his policy of increasing ferry subsidies (some 16% for 1983-84, distributed after scrutiny of the needs of each service) and that final commitment was still withheld.

THE CENTRAL SCOTLAND AIRPORTS

Although not complicated by political party commitments, the issues surrounding the central Scotland airports - Prestwick, Glasgow (Abbotsinch) and Edinburgh (Turnhouse) represent in Scottish terms an important exercise in policy formation and decision-making, because the rivalry between the supporters of the three airports is intense, and because an attempt was made to reach a firm decision after an unusually full exercise in open discussion. Policy was also made on the basis of purely Scottish considerations, although paradoxically enough in a field in which the Secretary of State for Scotland is not constitutionally responsible. Considerations relating to the rest of the UK, and in particular to Heathrow, Gatwick and the third London airport, played virtually no part in the argument.

Historically - and in the timescale of air transport the period since the end of the second world war represents a considerable historical span - the role of Glasgow

(1) 'The Government's reply to the Scottish Committee second report 1981-82': 4 October 1982

and Prestwick airports has been regarded by successive governments as complementary, Glasgow catering for short and medium haul traffic and Prestwick for inter-continental (i.e., transatlantic) traffic. Edinburgh developed somewhat separately. A small war-time airfield was allowed to develop as the airport for the capital city, since Glasgow airport was too far away (and involved at that time a journey through Glasgow's traffic blocks) to be acceptable, and Prestwick was even further. Increasing traffic and pressure for improvements led eventually to the building of the new runway and of the new terminal building in 1976 and 1977, which put an end to any possibility that the Edinburgh area might have to do without its own airport, just as at an earlier date the development of Abbotsinch, necessitated by increasing traffic and increasing size of aircraft, had virtually settled that Glasgow would continue to have its own airport for internal and European services. The construction of urban motorways past Abbotsinch, while the first part of the journey to Prestwick continued to be through city streets, also set the seal on this. Prestwick's long runway, its relative freedom from fog, and the fact that aircraft noise affected fewer people, ensured its development as a transatlantic airport, and there was intense local support for it because of the employment it generated and the industrial development it was felt to promote.

The growth of all three airports can therefore be said to have been determined by local considerations. A single airport would have sufficed to meet traffic needs, and for a time was vigorously advocated (particularly by the Edinburgh suburban communities who objected to the noise which they would endure from the new Edinburgh runway, even though other suburbs would benefit).

Given the investment put into the existing airports, and the resistance of Glasgow and Edinburgh air travellers, a single airport was never a starter, and was specifically ruled out by the Government's White Paper on Airport Policy of February 1978 (Cmnd.7084). The supporters of Glasgow and Edinburgh airports continued to press for development, and the supporters of Prestwick to guard against closure or restriction of functions. Edinburgh, in particular, mounted a case for inter-continental status, as the airport for the capital city, and this was vigorously pursued by speeches, letters, and Parliamentary activity, in spite of firm statements (for example, by Norman Payne, chairman of BAA, to the Consultative Committee for Edinburgh airport in January 1978) that transatlantic air services must continue to be handled at Prestwick. Even without intercontinental traffic, Edinburgh was the only one of the three airports whose usage was growing, and growing rapidly.

The relatively low level of traffic at Prestwick, and the manifest preference of the airlines for a single airport in the west of Scotland, which would make 'inter-lining' (e.g., the change from a transatlantic flight to a British or European flight) much easier, increased fears that Prestwick might be abandoned as a major civil airport. In September 1978 Strathclyde regional council were sufficiently concerned to ask for a deputation to meet Clinton Davis, then the Minister responsible for civil aviation, to express their concern over Prestwick, and Prestwick Airport Aviation Group emphasised that £50 million would have to be spent on Glasgow and Edinburgh airports to render them suitable for intercontinental flights.

The government had decided to take the line that any change in the roles of the airports should be left to the then proposed Scottish assembly to consider. In the course of 1978 British Airways Authority nevertheless decided to invite re-examination of the issues at a conference, so that "when the policy issues are finally decided, they will be resolved against the spectrum of informed opinion".

The extensive documentation provided for this was an excellent example of the best type of public consultation. Statistics and factual statements were provided for each of the three airports on passenger traffic, noise complaints, aircraft routeing procedures, and a number of other matters, amounting to over 100 pages of data in a clearly structured form, but the main document was a memorandum setting out at length the three possible options which BAA thought merited discussion. These were based on assumptions about traffic growth (the largest growth being expected in long haul traffic, both cargo and passenger) and the capital expenditure required to cater for the increased traffic in the way of airport facilities. Also estimated were the employment generated or lost, the date before the airports would break even, and the effect on disturbance by noise.

Option A was the status quo, with no freedom to aircraft operators to go outside this. Option B was freedom for charter flight operators to use the airports of their choice, and Option C was freedom for both charter operators and scheduled service airlines to use their preferred airports.

The analysis of the effect of each of these options was thorough and reads convincingly, even though some of it was necessarily a matter of judgment rather than of fact - for example, the redistribution of charter flights and (under Option C) scheduled flights between the airports if freedom of choice were allowed. In conclusion BAA summarised the advantages and disadvantages of the three options: Option A would require the least capital expenditure and produce the best net cash flow, and would keep Prestwick open for weather diversions and training (and, although BAA did not say so, would give the least satisfaction to the Edinburgh lobby). Option B, free choice for charter flights, would be more costly and less profitable, and BAA did not think it would be sustainable, in view of pressure from schedule airlines to be given the same freedom as charter operators. Option C, total freedom of choice, would require the greatest capital expenditure because of the improvements needed at Glasgow to cater for the increased traffic. To keep Prestwick open while giving freedom of choice of airport would reduce the net cash flow. Against the financial disadvantages of Options B and C and the loss of employment at Prestwick had to be set the shorter journey times for the majority of long-distance passengers.

BAA concluded by pointing out that in previous reviews their preference had been for the status quo. The further review was being carried out in the light of changes to the factors involved in the analysis. What these changes were is not clear: there was nothing in the mass of data produced to suggest that they could have been more than marginal. However BAA seem to have felt that the tensions between the three airports' supporters (and possibly tension within BAA itself) could only be resolved, or held in check, by a thorough re-examination of all the facts and arguments.

The proceedings at the conference, on 20 November 1978, were predictable: Prestwick's supporters advocated the status quo, and utilised all the material in BAA's documentation about employment in the area and about the facilities already provided at Prestwick to support it. The east of Scotland interests advocated freedom of choice to use Edinburgh airport while declaring themselves innocent of any wish to undermine Prestwick. British Airways were unequivocally in favour of locating transatlantic services at Glasgow. The Confederation of British Industry and the Scottish Council (Development and Industry) claimed that air services to Scotland could be improved but, as befits organisations with interests all over Scotland, were more cautious in recommending drastic changes. The Scottish Tourist Board thought that the market for holidays in Scotland could be developed by a proper airports policy, which in their view meant channelling all intercontinental scheduled services to Glasgow and all intercontinental charter flights to Prestwick.

The chairman at the end of the conference, Sir Kenneth Alexander, said he thought that the BAA options had not survived unscathed, but when BAA published a summary of the proceedings it included a report on action taken on the issues identified for future study; and they clearly thought those issues were side-issues which left the main options intact. However, by that time (March 1979) it was no longer possible to talk of leaving the decision to the Scottish assembly, and BAA left the whole matter in the lap of the Department of Trade and the Scottish Office, who had been kept in touch throughout.

The indications are that BAA wanted the government to take responsibility for deciding on future policy, perhaps because any decision (whether the status quo or a major charge) would be unpopular with somebody or other, but also because this would help to commit the government to authorising any additional capital expenditure and new financial targets involved. But the government proved unwilling to pick this chestnut out of the fire: the decision, in their view, should be that of the British Airways Authority itself. What happened, after a delay for consideration until December 1979, was the issue of a statement that Scottish Office and Department of Trade Ministers concurred in a decision of BAA that "the most economic proposition for the foreseeable future is to continue operating all three of Scotland's lowland airports as complementary to each other".

TRANSPORT POLICIES

It has been suggested more than once that the decision to maintain the status quo, and thus save Prestwick, was influenced by the fact that the airport is in the constituency of George Younger and adjoins that of Willie Ross, as his title of Lord Marnock recalls. This is too simplistic a view, and is unfair to the steps taken by BAA to publish all the evidence and engender discussion on the basis of it. One can speculate that the government might not have been so insistent on leaving the decision to BAA if there had been any danger of their reaching a different one, but given strict cash limits there was no real danger of that.

So the outcome of BAA's policy-making exercise was a decision, confirmed by the government, not to change policy. But it remains an interesting example of a Scottish decision taken without the pressure of English or UK arguments on the basis of public consultation, and of the self-cancelling effect of conflicting pressure groups.

Given the existence of two other major airports more closely situated to Glasgow in one case and Edinburgh in the other, it is unlikely that the arguments will ever die down completely. Since the 1979 decision was made, it has had to be reaffirmed on several occasions not only by departmental Ministers but also by the Prime Minister, who was asked what view she took of a paper by the Bow Group saying that Prestwick should be abandoned (the answer being that the Bow Group, however Conservative, is not the government). Then in September 1981 British Airways, who had always made plain their dislike of having to operate from Prestwick, abandoned both their passenger and their freight services out of the airport, thus cutting its income by about 12%. George Younger who had not heard of this in advance could not influence the decision, especially as it was taken on the grounds of reducing losses in a nationalised industry, but he obtained assurances from the British Airports Authority that as far as it was concerned Prestwick remained the transatlantic airport, and would have nearly £2 million spent on the runway.

There was a further blow to Prestwick when Laker Airlines, so far from increasing their use of the airport as they had proposed when British Airways withdrew, collapsed completely. These two events more than doubled the year's loss on the airport, but the BAA stood by their policy, though only because building up any other airport to intercontinental standard would be prohibitively expensive. All through this Glasgow Chamber of Commerce continud to insist that Prestwick must give way to Glasgow airport, and Edinburgh interests, while ingenuously disclaiming any desire to harm Prestwick, continued to demand that Edinburgh airport should have transatlantic services. The policy of maintaining Prestwick as Scotland's intercontinental airport, so painfully hammered out by BAA and approved by the Department of Trade and the Scottish Office, continued to hold the field, but the champions of Prestwick can hardly feel that events are favouring them.

CHAPTER V

INNER CITY PROBLEMS

There is a long history of concern over the problems of the Scottish cities - particularly the great conurbation centred on Glasgow - and in some major respects public policy has been strongly influenced by city questions. This is true in the fields of housing, planning, transport, economic development and social welfare, even to some extent in the realm of education, and very notably in the field of local government organisation. This does not mean that the needs of the cities have been regarded as paramount, but that the relationship of the cities and their surrounding regions has been at the centre of many policy decisions given the position of the cities as the core of each region's industrial and business structure, its transport system, its shopping patterns, its professional services, and its social and leisure provision.

THE REVOLUTION IN URBAN POLICIES

Within the city region, the problems of the older urban core have tended to dominate, because of the size of the population involved, the intensity of the housing problem, and the changes in city-centred industries. While these factors have persisted with little change for a generation or more, or have changed only by gradual evolution, the response in terms of public policies has been utterly transformed in that time. If such a complex series of changes can be summarised in one sentence, it might be said that a policy of clearance and decanting from the centre had been expected to lead to economic rejuvenation of the cities which had been thought to be held back only by the existence of so much congestion and dereliction; but as this did not happen the accepted policy turned decisively towards rehabilitation, social reconstruction, and how to retain the remaining inhabitants.

Paradoxically, the now despised policy of clearance and 'overspill' was valid, and indeed inevitable at the time, because the physical condition and congestion of the slum houses, slum schools, and slum factories were such that no improvement could be expected until space was created for redevelopment along healthier lines. People and politicians in the 1950s and 1960s are not to be condemned for favouring clearance and redevelopment, for promoting the new towns and encouraging overspill to other small towns; it was the only thing to do, and was accompanied by considerable successes, in particular the rebuilding of so many town centres, the achievement of the new towns in attracting new industries, and the considerable improvement in housing conditions (although that has been marred by the design faults in so many of the new houses built and the social problems created by the size and design of the new estates).

Nevertheless clearance proved easier than redevelopment, particularly as the latter was essentially dependent on securing an adequate share of the United Kingdom's economic growth, which faltered and stopped. In the space of a very few years, the view prevailed that there should be no more demolition, except for the worst of buildings, and that people must be persuaded to stay instead of encouraged to leave. Although in earlier years much of the clearance of the older city areas had been planned, notably the 29 comprehensive development areas in Glasgow and a few others elsewhere, much of the emptying of the cities had, as elsewhere in Britain, taken place without deliberate direction by central or local government. Huge areas of city tenements had begun to fall down because it was not worthwhile for the landlords to maintain them, and wholesale demolition by the local authorities became inevitable. With them went the shops - with the notable exception of the pubs - and the old schools and other public buildings. Meanwhile industrial changes were leading to the closure of factories and workshops as the buildings and the products for which they were designed became obsolete.

INNER CITY PROBLEMS

The process of decline fed upon itself; the more an area became run-down, the less attractive it was to new enterprises, and the more those who could leave did so the less were those who remained qualified to fill the jobs that were still available. This last point was and still is one of the greatest paradoxes of the inner area problem - those areas, in spite of decline, continue to provide employment for the city and its region as a whole, but to an increasing extent those who still live in the area are old, disabled, and unskilled and therefore unable to compete for the available jobs with those who travel into the inner city to work every day. This is a prime factor in the social disintegration of the community which remains.

THE MAGNITUDE OF THE GLASGOW PROBLEM

The inner area problems of all cities are acute; the phenomena of dereliction, demolition, loss of skilled and active population, and the decay of local industries are familiar in Edinburgh and Dundee, and to a lesser extent in Aberdeen, while many of the larger towns also have areas displaying similar features. But the very size of Glasgow's zone of dereliction makes it different in kind, because its population is physically isolated from the rest of the city to a much greater extent than elsewhere, and because social and economic collapse on such a large scale requires inordinately greater efforts to deal with it. Glasgow has been spared the racial tensions and the major problems of public order which afflict so many cities in England, but in all other respects the city figures all too high on the indicators of 'multiple deprivation' such as overcrowding, inadequate housing, and high proportions of unskilled workers, the elderly, the disabled, and one-parent families.

A large number of mainly small schemes for improvement of social conditions were started with the aid of the special government grant - urban aid - given under the Local Government Grants (Social Needs) Act 1969, and with the help of rate support grant and housing subsidies the local authorities continued to operate very considerable social, educational and rehousing programmes. But this did not match the rate of decline, in spite of a consensus of opinion between central and local government that the most deprived areas should be given preference in the allocation of resources. In any case dealing with the immediate problems caused by the decline swallowed a large proportion of the money and manpower that was available.

Until the mid 1970s urban aid was the only government policy specifically directed towards helping inner urban areas. Both Labour and Tory administrations have been anxious to see this employed more widely, in other cities as well as Glasgow, but it is not a policy specifically designed for Scotland, and changes in it have to a large extent followed the line taken in England. Scotland's distinctive contribution to inner city policy was the measures adopted for eastern Glasgow.

GLASGOW EASTERN AREA RENEWAL

All parties were agreed about the severity of inner city problems, but the Labour party in course of time became more inclined than the Conservatives to see the resources devoted to the new towns as depriving the inner cities still further. It tended to regard the new towns not so much as centres of additional employment, new technologies, and national wealth, but as places which attracted jobs and people out of the cities. Under the Labour government of 1974 onwards there was bound to be a review of the new town programme, and the results of this appeared in May 1976, when Bruce Millan announced that the government agreed with Strathclyde regional council that the development of Stonehouse new town, the last in the Scottish series, would not be compatible with the strategy for the region. Stonehouse would therefore not proceed, thus endorsing a change of emphasis, he said, towards renewal of the older urban areas.

Discussions had been proceeding meanwhile on how that renewal, in relation to Glasgow, should be organised. From 1975 there were two local authorities on the scene instead of one - Strathclyde responsible for strategic planning, transport, education and social work, and Glasgow district responsible for local planning and housing. Relations between the two were marked by a certain prickliness, especially on the part of the district council, which tended to see itself as Glasgow Corporation stripped of many of its most important functions. There was an imperative need for co-operation, especially in the complex of problems posed by urban decline, but neither authority was inclined to concede the leading role to the other. The Scottish Office did not see itself as a co-ordinator in the executive sense of preparing plans and budgets, but there was an alternative in the shape of the recently created Scottish Development Agency, with existing powers to aid industry and undertake environmental improvements.

After a good deal of discussion it was agreed that the SDA should provide the 'co-ordinating management' of a project for the rejuvenation not of the whole of inner Glasgow, but a particular sector of it, the East End, extending from Glasgow Green to Cambuslang and Shettleston. The decision to concentrate on one geographical area was taken because of the magnitude of the problems of the inner city as a whole, and it was also hoped that the East End would act as a demonstration project for other areas and allow the local authorities to devote more attention to those other areas while some of the burden of dealing with the East End was taken from them.

The announcement of a new plan for the East End was made a few days after the news of the cancellation of Stonehouse new town; Bruce Millan described the area of 3,500 acres as containing some of the worst urban deprivation in western Europe and said that improvement would be effected not only by diverting some existing resources to it but also by putting in additional resources through the SDA and the Scottish Special Housing Association. The amount of additional resources was not stated, but a figure of £120m. having been mentioned as the total cost of the work to be done, the impression wrongly gained ground that most if not all of this was extra money. Bruce Millan gave an assurance that resources directed to the East End would not be at the expense of other parts of the city or of Strathclyde region. And although the switch of resources was not just because of the decision to abandon Stonehouse, the chairman of the SDA said that it was an opportunity to bring the new town technique into one of the most rundown areas in Scotland.

The new town technique of giving an appointed corporation the major responsibility for new construction work and allowing it to purchase land at a controlled price was not, however, adopted. Nor would it have been appropriate to an area where, in spite of decline, there were still so many factories and businesses, so many existing houses, and such a network of local authority buildings, schools and services. New Towns had worked because they developed largely on green-field sites, even where they were based on an existing town; the problems of renovating built-up areas were different and enormously greater. The new town technique might have worked if the local authorities had been willing to transfer their responsibilities to a new authority, but they were not, and to a large extent it would not have made sense to do so, because a slice of a city cannot have its services planned and provided, according to different priorities, separately from the rest of the city.

The terms of the agreement on the Glasgow east end project between the local authorities, the SDA, the SSHA, and the Secretary of State for Scotland, were like a treaty between sovereign states. There would be a governing committee of elected members with Hugh Brown as the initial chairman which would not in any real sense have governing powers. Its function, like that of the more accurately named consultative group of senior officials, was to serve as a forum for ideas, resolve points of difficulty, give directions or advice (powers to give directions could only relate to the Secretary of State's powers over the SDA and the SSHA), and be responsible for general progress; but each of the participants would retain its full statutory powers and remain responsible for the implementation of its own functions. The SDA was named as the co-ordinator, with responsibility for preparing plans and proposing budgets on the basis of the other participants' own proposals, but was given no executive authority over the other participants. Any other arrangement would have flaunted the realities of central-local relationships.

What had been created was a partnership, not a board of directors. (The term partnership was not explicitly used until, some months later, similar arrangements were established in several cities in England.) It proved a somewhat uneasy partnership, because each of the members, with varying degrees of emphasis, insisted on their own statutory rights and responsibilities, and some were inclined to hint that they could have done the whole job themselves if they had been left to get on with it without interference.

The project was not free of staffing problems, either; the Glasgow branch of the National Association of Local Government Officers saw the new organisation as taking bread out of their mouths by transferring work from the local authorities to the SDA, and were not easily reassured. It was true that in the early days the SDA had to recruit a considerable number of planning staff, but this was not at the expense of the range of local government activities: in fact the preparation of no less than 21 statutory local plans in the East End area continued unabated. Work on these plans, in particular the process of local consultation required by law, and the local consultation undertaken by the SDA in connection with the proposals they were drawing up, was later to cause some dissension.

The scheme soon came to be known as GEAR, the Glasgow Eastern Area Renewal project. This was a convenient acronym, which suggested something was happening. It also provided sub-editors in the Press however with an opportunity for headlines such as "One Speed Gear"; here as elsewhere in the papers headlines tended to be a good deal less balanced in their labelling of a topic than the articles which they headed.

The participants, in spite of their defence of their own territories, were sincere in their commitment to GEAR, and at the second meeting of the governing committee a quite impressive list of early objectives was drawn up. Most of these were in the field of environmental improvement and small factory building which were the sole responsibility of the SDA, and for which the SDA could expect the Scottish Office to provide the resources needed, since the government was anxious to make a success of its newly-created Agency. Apart from this, the function of the Scottish Office was that of any chairman of a meeting - to suggest topics for joint discussion, to persuade the participants to reach agreement on action to be taken, and to check up on the progress on those agreements.

Although Bruce Millan had claimed that the project was not just going to produce another plan, another plan was in fact necessary, and it fell to the SDA to draw it up, with information provided from the other participants on what was being done under their own policies. There was also a necessary, but some felt unduly prolonged, process of local consultation, for which consultative proposals first had to be drafted and agreed. It did not prove easy to shape these in a form which was both realistic and easy to get across, or to elicit what the reaction of the local communities really was. Attempts were made to enlist the attention of Glasgow's business community in the scheme, with indifferent success.

The rest of Glasgow was anxious to make sure that the GEAR area did not get preferential treatment. This was something which councillors in particular had to take account of, and it may well have helped to delay the rate of progress. Although taking on the whole of the inner city as the zone for a special partnership project would have been an enormous undertaking, it would have been easier to justify devoting special attention and resources to all the areas where inner city decline was occurring rather than just one of them.

While GEAR was getting under way, the government published a White Paper on policy for inner cities [(1)]. This was a UK policy, but one to which Scottish factors and experience contributed substantially. It extended to five inner areas of major cities partnership arrangements similar to those already adopted for the east end of Glasgow, contained an undertaking to increase urban programme grants three- or four-fold (most of the increase going to the partnership areas), extended those grants to include industrial, environmental, and recreational schemes as well as the social projects originally eligible, and said that rate support grant would continue to be distributed on lines which took account of local authorities with severe urban problems. (In money terms rate support grant was overwhelmingly the biggest source of government help to local authorities, even after the urban programme was tripled, but the value of the latter both to central and to local government was that as a grant for specific projects it could demonstrate their commitment to meeting special needs in the inner areas.)

The government, recognising that the minor changes possible in their distribution of industry policy were not enough to give it an adequate 'inner area dimension', promised legislation to give authorities with severe urban problems

(1) 'Policy for the Inner Cities', Cmnd 6845, June 1977

powers to offer loans to new industry and rent-free periods in the factories they provided, and to help with the cost of site preparation. Those proposals duly became law in the Inner Urban Areas Act, but were not of much relevance to GEAR, where the SDA was already in a position to give aid to industry.

A few months after the publication of the White Paper there was a series of television programmes of a novel, and as it proved, controversial kind which seem to have had a profound effect on public understanding of inner city conditions. This was the BBC's November 1977 programmes on 'Lilybank', not an area of ancient tenements but a run-down council house area in eastern Glasgow, which Kay Carmichael, deputy chairman of the Supplementary Benefits Commission, lived in for some time on supplementary benefit rates in order to experience life near the poverty line and the attitude of others to those living in an area labelled as one of the worst in the city.

A large audience for these programmes was guaranteed by two pieces of unexpected publicity - firstly the report that the BBC had considered adding sub-titles to translate the Glasgow dialect for showing in England and Wales, and secondly the court action taken, without success, by some of the residents to prevent the showing of the programmes. (The court decided that, as an assurance had been given that the complainer would not be named in the programmes, the public interest would best be served by allowing them to be shown.)

After the showing, headlines like "Shocking 'spy' scenes from life in Lilybank" ensured that controversy would continue. Although Glasgow District Councillors thought the programmes caused damage and degradation, and although newspaper reports indicated that Mrs Carmichael was thought by the head of her university department to have committed an error of judgment, the bulk of comments published in the Press strongly commended what she and the BBC had done. It was described as an important piece of television journalism, and commended as outspoken and uncensored, and it is clear from the daily papers' letter columns for some weeks afterwards that the programmes had engendered a massive debate on the problems not only of Lilybank, but of other problem housing areas, a debate between those who thought the programmes positively harmful to deprived people, and those who maintained that they had not caused degradation, but just brought to light. In any event, it can hardly be doubted that television had brought to the notice of hundreds of thousands of people who might never experience it at first hand what inner city life could be like.

In the Spring of 1983 the BBC televised another series of programmes about the inner area and the wider economic problems of Glasgow. At the time of writing it is not possible to say whether these will engender a similar debate to that on 'Lilybank'.

INNER CITY POLICY UNDER THE CONSERVATIVES

There had never been any substantial disagreement between the political parties about the problems and dangers of the inner city situation. During their last year or two in opposition, however, the Conservatives sketched policies of urban regeneration which modified their inner city policy. The first was Sir Geoffrey Howe's proposal, made public at a Bow Group meeting in London's Isle of Dogs in 1978, for no-control, no-subsidy areas where regeneration might take place precisely because of the withdrawal of government supervision. This idea, which may or may not have been inspired by Peter Hall's freeport area proposals of 1977, was something which Howe was in a position to promote when he became Chancellor of the Exchequer, although he had to move towards extra financial incentives in place of freedom to operate without controls.

The story of what became known, in a well-chosen phrase, as 'enterprise zones', has been given elsewhere[1]. Although the scheme was eagerly taken up by George Younger's administration, it was not adopted for the GEAR area, in spite of being, in its modified form, much more akin to GEAR and other inner cities' schemes than it had been at first. As a different kind of social experiment it made sense to establish a Scottish enterprise zone in a different area, and it might not have been safe or practicable to give rates and tax concessions and partial withdrawal of planning control to such a large area as GEAR. The enterprise zone concept became something to apply to relatively small areas, not something for inner cities as a whole. Special programmes of environmental

---

(1) Jordan & Reilly, Scottish Government Year Book 1982, Edinburgh

improvement and factory building were set up in Leith, Motherwell, and other areas, on a joint basis between the SDA and the local authorities, but these were more akin to GEAR than to enterprise zones.

The second Conservative proposal was to set up urban development corporations on the analogy of the highly successful new town corporations. They would have specific building and promotional responsibilities, and their more extreme supporters thought of them as supplanting the local authorities of the area for a wide range of services. The idea of applying this scheme to GEAR was pressed with some force in Conservative circles, and caused alarm to the local authorities in the GEAR project who (to quote the chief executive of Glasgow district) thought that urban development corporations would sow the seeds of destruction of local government. It was not, however, a possibility mentioned by Malcolm Rifkind at the first meeting of the GEAR governing committee which he attended in June 1979, a meeting which preserved the continuity of activity on GEAR projects notwithstanding the change of government.

In the following months the Scottish Office formally consulted the region and district councils for their views on urban development corporations, and received an unequivocal rejection, both Labour and Tory councillors being opposed to the idea that a new authority could do any better, or that one sector of the city could be sliced off and administered separately. At the next meeting of the governing committee in May 1980 Malcolm Rifkind announced that the government would not insist on an urban development corporation because of the two councils' objections and because it might delay progress which was already being made.

The GEAR project was thus readopted by the new government without any changes in principle. At the 1980 meeting the participants, without too much acrimony about the public spending cuts being imposed by the government, agreed their spending commitments in the area for 1980-81 and the basic strategy for the area proposed by the SDA.

It had taken four years to reach this point, but considering the complex physical and social structure of the area, the severity of its problems, and the number of public authorities concerned who had to reconcile GEAR with their other responsibilities, this was not bad going. There was no further meeting of the governing committee for over a year, which suggests that GEAR was now a continuing project which did not arouse the suspicions and arguments that it had once done. It was reported at the 1981 meeting that the agreed public sector programmes had been fulfilled so far; the unanswered question was whether the economic and social decline of the area had been stemmed.

The indications were not hopeful: although the GEAR area was still a major employment area (almost more for the rest of Glasgow than for its own inhabitants) jobs in manufacturing industry were declining at a terrifying rate as products, and the premises in which they were manufactured, came to the end of their life period; as increasing automation in the remaining factories produced a lessening need for labour; and as the economic recession took hold. Against this tide the number of new jobs, largely in factories and workshops provided by the SDA, had little effect. The proportion of the unskilled and the least employable sections of the work force remained high in spite of retraining. Population continued to decline through clearance and voluntary movement, and the very popular rehabilitated houses and the small amount of new housebuilding could not do much to offset this. The outward appearance of the area was beginning to improve considerably, because environmental improvement was a policy which was largely within the ability of the SDA, the SSHA, and the local authorities to command, and was favourably treated in the government's expenditure plans. An air of desolation, though less now of dereliction, continued to exist because of the large amount of vacant land; with the demolition of vast areas of tenements and nineteenth-century factories, the availability of land was much greater than the demand for it.

Both in GEAR, and through the rest of urban Scotland, priority was given by the Conservative government, in the urban grants programme, to schemes which "mobilised private sector resources" or used vacant land, but the majority of schemes were public or community enterprises. By and large, the attempt to get private capital reinvested in the area has not been successful; even industrial and commercial projects had to be led by the Scottish

Development Agency, as in the adaptation of the former Templeton's carpet factory (the 'Doge's palace') as a business centre for both offices and workshops.

However limited the success of the policies adopted, there is no obvious alternative to continuing them and modifying them at the margin; neither GEAR nor any other inner city area can be abandoned to decay, and over a sufficiently long time-scale economic and social changes throughout the country, such as the increasing cost of transport and commuting to work, may turn in favour of the inner areas. If so, the policy of partnership between central government, local government, and public agencies, which was first conceived and adopted in Scotland, will be shown to have made an essential contribution to the rescue process.

CHAPTER VI

CONCLUSIONS

This book has been an attempt to discover, in the field of environmental politics in the last few years in Scotland, the sources of public policy and to assess the strengths of the various agencies contributing to decisions on policy. It is now time to consider whether it is possible to draw any general conclusions. There are many hypotheses from which to choose - that public policy is the result of the struggle between conflicting pressure groups; that policies develop in an evolutionary fashion and are only adopted to the extent that the community regards them as feasible and legitimate; that the influence of the press, radio, and television is paramount; that civil servants determine what happens behind the frontage of Ministerial control. Against these theories is the orthodox theory of Cabinet responsibility with an executive drawn from and dependent on Parliament and ultimately responsible to the electorate.

The background against which these hypotheses must be assessed in relation to Scottish affairs is the fact that in matters of government Scotland is part of the United Kingdom, not a self-governing, or even partly self-governing, community. Despite the presence of the Scottish Office in Edinburgh, and the existence of various independent Scottish pressure groups, political parties, newspapers and television companies, and the separate Scottish legal system, no policy can be considered - still less adopted - without ultimately the agreement or acceptance by UK organs of government. The political parties, with the exception of the Scottish National Party, are parts of a Great Britain political structure, most pressure groups have British affiliations, most of the media are owned or organised on a UK level, the civil service is part of the UK civil service, and the ultimate power resides with a UK executive, a UK Parliament, and a UK electorate.

WHAT DEVOLUTION MIGHT HAVE BROUGHT

During the later 'seventies the most intense political debate by far in Scotland was on whether devolution would allow a limited number of policies - including the environmental matters with which this book is concerned - to be determined by a Scottish assembly and executive. The results of the referendum, held under the 40% rule, and the subsequent repeal of the Scotland Act rendered this debate abortive, and discussions as to what policies would have been adopted by a devolved administration must be speculative.

But the voting patterns in the 1979 general election, coming so soon after the defeat of devolution, make it possible to guess with some assurance what would have happened. Even if the Labour government had not been defeated in May 1979, there would have been a general election a few months later, and there is no reason to suppose that the Conservatives would not have had a working majority in UK terms. Equally there is no reason to suppose, in the light of the actual voting patterns, that the elections to the Scottish assembly, due to be held shortly afterwards, would have returned a Tory majority. A non-Conservative assembly would therefore have had to deal with a Conservative government at Westminster with control over the total amount of resources allocated to Scotland and the immediate consequence of this would have been a running dispute about public expenditure.

We can assume that the Tory Cabinet would have allocated to Scotland funds not exceeding those actually allocated to the Scottish Office since 1979, involving a substantial cut in services which were not guaranteed against cuts by the party manifesto. The Scottish executive and assembly would have had to decide how this was to be borne but it is difficult to see what alternative they would have had to taking it mainly on the public sector housing programme, as in England. Only the education, health and housing programmes deal with enough money to find within themselves savings of the scale required, and adequate savings could not have been made in the first two without a drastic reduction of standards and widespread redundancies. The roads and transport programme could not have contributed enough without some such device as dropping the entire road construction programme.

In all probability, therefore, the executive would have had to make on local housing authorities much the same demands for higher rents or smaller building programmes as the Conservative government has done in actual fact. If the local authorities had refused to put up their rents enough the executive would have had little choice but to reduce their capital allocations still further, since the block grant from Whitehall would not have expanded to meet the deficit. Housing policies such as council tenants' security of tenure would probably have been implemented, since there was inter-party agreement on them and they do not cost anything. It is highly unlikely, however, that there would have been a majority in the assembly for the compulsory sale of council houses to tenants who wished to buy. Unlike the situation with regard to rents and capital expenditure, financial considerations would not have forced the assembly to give way, since it would not have cost anything in money terms to deny the right of purchase to tenants. It is in this field that there would have been the greatest divergence between Scottish and English policies, with much greater harmony between the central and local authorities in Scotland but correspondingly greater resentment on the part of some Scottish council tenants that they did not have the right to buy.

In other fields of environmental policy, whether land use, transport, countryside or inner city issues, it is not likely that devolution would have led to a vastly different set of policies than the ones actually followed by the Conservative government. There are two reasons for this; firstly the control of the purse by Whitehall, which as in housing would have prevented big new expenditure programmes (as on rail and public transport, for example, which a non-Conservative assembly might have favoured), and secondly the fact that on other environmental issues the divisions between the parties such as exist on housing matters are not nearly so deep, and the Scottish executive would have taken decisions on the circumstances of each case, like any other government dealing with non-party issues. It is difficult to envisage a Scottish executive, for example, deciding to enforce much stricted (or for that matter much more relaxed) control over development, or slashing the road programme to pay for huge rail and bus investment, scrapping urban aid and the GEAR project, or making big cuts in the water and sewerage programme.

Irrespective of what might have happened in the other main programmes controlled by the assembly, it is therefore pretty certain that the housing policy in itself would have led to a permanent confrontation between the Scottish assembly and executive on the one hand, and the government on the other. The former would have taken every possible opportunity to show their resentment about the inadequate resources allotted to them, just as most housing authorities have done since 1979, but of course on a much greater scale and with strongly nationalistic overtones.

The position of the Secretary of State and of the residual Scottish Office would in this situation have been not only politically but constitutionally difficult. In terms of the Scotland Act the Secretary of State and his staff in Edinburgh would not have had any specific responsibility for the monetary allocations, as these would have been a decision of the government as a whole, but it is not difficult to imagine that there would have been constant and intense pressure on the Secretary of State to receive deputations, consider representations, and permit discussions among officials about the effects of the public expenditure policy being forced upon the assembly and executive. No doubt the Secretary of State would have acceded to those requests to some extent, though it is not likely that there could have been any real dialogue, still less any significant concessions by the government. And so long as voting patterns are as different in Scotland and England as they were in the 1979 general election, any future devolved authority in Scotland is likely to be in dispute with the government unless it has a stronger influence over the financial resources it commands.

THE PRESSURE GROUPS

After this brief speculation on the possible short-term effects of devolution on environmental policies, let us return to the analysis of events as they actually occurred, to see if they support or suggest any principles by which policy is adopted.

The expansion in the number and size of pressure groups suggests that they must be thought effective by their members in influencing government policy, and certainly a large number of them are consulted by the Scottish Office, as the chapters on housing and transport in particular have shown. The Scottish Office, at both official and ministerial level, regard this process as a necessary and welcome means of getting advice on the different views held throughout the country, and bringing to light detailed defects or anomalies in circulated proposals. The drafting of legislation would be impossible without consultation of this kind and the detailed changes in legislation which ensue.

It is in this respect that COSLA functions most effectively, that is not as a pressure group with a policy to advocate, but as a commentator on the draft schemes, bills, and regulations which local authorities will have to administer when in force. This is the nearest approach in our field to a corporatist arrangement, where an organisation has a virtual monopoly in representing its members' views to government, and is specially recognised by the government in this role. Neither the STUC nor the Scottish office of the CBI can lay claim to a position like this in environmental matters. Severe strain has been put on this relationship by events in the field of rate support grant in the last two or three years, but these are beyond the scope of this book.

The success of other pressure groups in promoting their causes is mixed. Shelter, in relation to homelessness, forced the government to change its mind on a major issue, but had no significant effect two or three years later on the main housing policies of a determined Tory administration. None of the transport pressure groups could sway either the Labour or the Tory administration to their exclusive point of view, and they were in any case pulling in different directions. Within limits, however, the balance of power between different pressure groups in the transport field does influence policy, because apart from issues of dogma such as nationalisation and privatisation governments are willing to listen to the many competing interest groups and to take account of what they say in deciding the level of investment in different modes of transport. Even so, Conservatives' preference for private enterprise tends to make them look with greater favour on a large roads programme, and it was this, rather than the power of pressure groups, which enabled the roads programme to escape some of the post-1979 cuts.

Local pressure groups have been effective where they have not set their aspirations too high and where they were in a position to use the procedure of a statutory public inquiry to put across their point of view. The local opponents of the Crow Road expressway achieved their aim in this way, and the Aberdour and Dalgety Bay Joint Action Group, even if they could not in the end stop the Moss Morran gas and petrochemical plan, helped to ensure by their persistence that an elaborate set of conditions relating to safety and the protection of the environment was attached to the planning permission. The groups opposing Torness nuclear power station could not prevent work starting on it in spite of reduced predictions about the demand for electricity. Orkney interests did not succeed in getting a permanent ban on uranium prospecting.

But it was in the field of nuclear power that pressure groups, both local and national, secured their greatest success, the virtual abandonment of field research into disposing of nuclear waste underground, where they were aided by the unwillingness of Ministers to force through a highly unpopular programme of research whose benefits, if any, were in the distant future. Pressure groups in other words are like the weaker pieces on a chessboard: they can easily be picked off, but if adequately supported they can force a checkmate.

THE MEDIA

It is difficult to find evidence, in the environmental field, that press, radio and television exert strong influence, or indeed set themselves out to do so, except on rare occasions, since they give much less prominence to environmental topics than to employment, inflation, labour affairs, and a multitude of other subjects. But of course any coverage, however limited, given to pressure groups' criticisms of government policy, often framed in such terms as mismanagement, failure, wrong-headedness and cover-ups, is one of the main means by which groups exert their influence. Ministers and civil servants are well accustomed to assessing the weight to be given to a newspaper article or a television programme, depending on whether it represents just the views of the newspaper or a particular correspondent or those of influential groups in the community. The effect of news selection is endlessly argued, and difficult to prove, but in environmental affairs deliberate selection does not seem to play a large part in what is published except on the not very frequent occasions when a paper has decided to mount a campaign on a national environmental issue.

THE CIVIL SERVANTS

Relationships between Ministers and their officials are a matter of confidence, but officials exert influence by the presentation of the relevant facts and the available options in any given situation and by advocating one option rather than another. This is their proper function and one without which Ministers would find it difficult to reach decisions on the very wide range of matters which are submitted to them. Moreover, as Malcolm Rifkind has related (1), official advice takes account of known policy directives, whether in manifestos or other Ministerial commitments. If the Ministers in an administration have an open mind on new policies, official thinking plays a large part in the drafting of consultative documents, such as the Housing Green Paper, the papers on possible changes in planning control, and the consultation paper on island ferry subsidies. But when there is a firm Ministerial line it is incorporated, as in the consultation papers issued on the new government's proposals in 1979 for tenants' rights and the sale of council houses. If there is already a party or Ministerial commitment it is for the civil servants to advise how it can be met. This must include drawing attention to

---

(1) Scottish Government Year Book 1982

the costs, financial and otherwise, and the undesirable side-effects of a policy, but this is not obstructionism.

Nor does the Treasury play the wicked uncle role still often assigned to it. Treasury officials are concerned with methods of cost-control and getting the best value for money, but they do not concern themselves with individual projects to the same extent as in the past, and even when it comes to settling the main expenditure programmes of the Scottish Office the Treasury is less involved than it used to be since over much of the field the limit nowadays is a fixed proportion of the UK total.

MONEY CONSTRAINTS

This last comment is not intended to show that finance has an insignificant role in policy-making. On the contrary, any policy which costs money, or through which substantial savings could be made, depends on the amount of resources available for it. Under both Labour and Tory administrations this has been a crucial factor in spite of the difference in the two governments' motives (control of public expenditure being a regrettable necessity to the Labour government, but an end in itself to the Conservatives).

In the environmental field, housing, as the biggest spender, is the area in which financial considerations are of most importance, and the last ten years have seen a dramatic decline in the amount of public money devoted to it. But even so this was not, under Labour, the consequence of a deliberate policy so much as of local authorities' decisions on the level of their housing programmes.

As regards roads, the next biggest environmental programme, both governments had to cut back, but neither was seriously hindered from doing what it wanted to do in the long run by lack of finance; both maintained a substantial construction programme and most projects which either administration was keen on were incorporated within it, though often several years later than originally planned. Other important environmental programmes such as grants for historic buildings and the care of ancient monuments, which have not featured in this book because they are not major areas of policy debate, have survived with only minor cuts due to financial constraints.

THE FINAL ARBITER

It is indisputable that the overall effect of the responsibilities of office, financial constraints, and the advice of departmental officials is to file away the rough edges of party policy. But it does not follow that policy changes are always evolutionary in character. The election of 1979 is one of the clearest refutations of this idea. Ideas such as enterprise zones, a blitz on quangos, freedom from planning control, and road equivalent tariffs to the islands were toned down a good deal when the incoming Ministers saw the problems from the inside but the radical changes in policy - the new attitude towards public expenditure and the commitment to give council tenants the right to buy their houses - were achieved without any fundamental revision. The reason is, of course, not difficult to find: the support of the majority at Westminster for those two articles of Tory faith.

Indeed on this occasion, as earlier, the model which best represents the reality of how policies have been determined in Scotland is the classical one of Ministers responsible to Parliament, Party and ultimately the electorate.

This is not a fashionable conclusion. It is commonly said that the government's responsibility to Parliament is nominal, that Ministers dragoon their back-benchers to suit themselves, that MPs have no influence, and that governments manipulate the electorate. The instances which support this do not add up to a refutation of the democratic pattern, certainly not within the specific field of study we have been dealing with (with the important proviso that what ultimately counts is not the vote of Scotland, but the vote of the UK). Bruce Millan's policies, much reshaped through the experience of office, most notably in the housing field, depended, as did the future of the Labour government, on the careful management of Labour back-bench support and the retention of Liberal and SNP support or neutrality. When this failed the government as a whole was defeated. The policies of George Younger's administration were determined by the Conservative election manifesto, the support given to it at a UK level by the electorate, and the unanimity within the Tory party. Furthermore, these policies were, within the environmental field, very largely within the power of a government to achieve, since they did not require additional resources - the bugbear of so many Labour policies - and were of a kind which could be brought about by legislation or executive controls. Thus under both governments, all other factors, whether the media, the pressure groups, or the resistance of established interests, were secondary to the role of Parliament and the electorate.

POSTSCRIPT

THE ENVIRONMENT AND THE 1983 ELECTION

In environmental as in other matters the advent of the general election in June 1983 required the political parties to redefine their policies, starting (in the case of the Conservatives) from what they had achieved in four years, and (as regards the opposition parties) on the basis of the changes they wanted to make to the trends set by the Tories. With the exception of housing, which as on previous occasions got a fair degree of attention, environmental policies got a respectable rather than a prominent showing in the manifestos of the major parties and in television, radio and press coverage, but they are the only bases of assessment that will be available until a considerable time after the election for an assessment of the future course of environmental affairs.

Though an outsider might well have been able to sketch the outlines of the manifestos himself from a knowledge of party attitudes, and though in general they contained few surprises, it is the precise wording of the manifestos which tends to reveal the reality of the promises made and the commitments undertaken, the need to get agreement within the party, and the extent to which parties emphasise the more popular and gloss over the less popular aspects of their policies. The tone of manifestos differs radically, of course, between the party in government and parties in opposition - the former's being essentially a vindication of its achievements and a promise to do more and better, and the latters' an outright attack on the policies of the last few years (or in the case of the Alliance on those of both Tory and Labour).

THE ENVIRONMENT AND THE 1983 ELECTION

With these considerations in mind let us look first at the environmental policies set out in the Labour Party manifesto. With Labour opposed to practically everything the Tories had done in the field of housing, it is not surprising that the party included in its emergency programme an undertaking to increase housing investment programmes by 50%; though the undertaking to freeze all rents for a year suggested that the problems of housing finance created by a similar promise carried out in the 1970s did not weigh very heavily with the party's policy-makers. (Civil servants and local government officers who would have to put party manifestos into operation do not write them.) The manifesto promised, as regards council houses, to repeal the right to buy, although this was euphemistically described as ending enforced council house sales, and to end the discount on sales where, in future, they took place on a voluntary agreed basis. A little more surprising, as a potential vote-loser, was the undertaking to give local authorities the right of repurchase on first resale, with encouraging reassurances to the owners about the method of valuation. As regards privately-rented houses, the idea that local authorities should take them all over ('municipilisation' to use a once fashionable term) resurfaced, in the form of a carefully worded promise to 'actively encourage' the transfer, with local authorities 'setting the pace'. Did this mean compulsory purchase, and at what price? We shall never know. More straightforward was the expected promise to repeal the short tenancy scheme and by implication give those tenants full security of tenure - a threat which (as pointed out earlier in this book, does much to render the scheme ineffective even though the Labour party did not get the chance to put its policy into effect.)

On other housing issues, there was more similarity between the Labour and Tory policies than either party would probably care to admit, if one looks at the actual proposals rather than the tone in which they were described. For example, the Labour party proposed to give tenants 'the right to force landlords, including councils, to get routine repairs done, with landlords footing the cost'. This is not really very different from the Conservative promise to 'extend our Tenants' Charter to enable council tenants to get necessary repairs done themselves and be reimbursed by their councils', apart from the fact that this notably did not apply to tenants of private landlords. Both parties wanted to get empty council houses brought back into use (with the emphasis on selling for owner-occupation in the case of the Tories) and to improve council estates. Similarly both parties wanted to use the building societies more in pursuance of their housing policies, though with subtle differences of emphasis which could have proved important, for while the Tories proposed 'consultation on proposals which would enable the building societies to play a fuller part in supporting the provision of new housing', the Labour manifesto said that mortgages for lower income groups should be 'financed primarily by on-lending from building societies, at least 10% of whose funds should be made available in this way'. What degree of pressure or even compulsion lay behind those words was not explained.

Both parties - indeed all parties - appeared as advocates for home ownership. The Labour party claimed that they had done more than any other to assist owner-occupiers, and promised to extend this by giving special assistance to first-time buyers (presumably by a development of the scheme introduced by the Labour government in the 1970s) and council tenants (who were nevertheless to lose the right to buy at a discount). The Tories said that most Scots want the security of owning their own homes, but apart from promising to ensure that land is available for private building the Tory manifesto concentrated once again on the right to buy council houses - what had been, and what more could be, achieved.

In the field of pollution policy there was little essential difference between the Labour and Conservative plans. The Labour party would 'proceed with the implementation' of the 1974 Control of Pollution Act (a process which had proved slow under either government), eliminate lead in petrol (a matter on which the Tories had already beaten them to the post by an announcement earlier in the year), and develop a programme for eliminating toxic substances from the environment. The Tory manifesto spoke of reducing lead in paints, food, and drinking water, as well as removing it from petrol; and promised to continue reducing river pollution, to support recycling and reclamation, and to tighten the controls on hazardous waste.

THE ENVIRONMENT AND THE 1983 ELECTION

Some aspects of transport policy, as might have been expected from the evidence of past decades, showed much more divergence, the main difference being between the Labour undertaking to improve and invest in the rail network, including electrification, and the Tory insistence that cost reductions and fewer restrictive practices were needed to justify investment. In regard to the environmental aspects of transport, the Labour manifesto took a tough line on the control of heavy lorries, by measures against noise and air pollution and by route restrictions, and promised better traffic management schemes and more by-passes (though these two latter objectives were hardly a matter of controversy between parties). The Labour manifesto was also strong on planning matters, preparing yet another scheme for the acquisition of land for development at its current value, environmental reports on major developments, greater resources for the countryside and wildlife, and environmental and planning controls over agriculture.

Before considering the course which the Tory administration in Scotland is likely to follow in environmental matters, we should look briefly at the proposals of three other parties, recognising that they will have no power to influence policies except by persuasion. There was a good deal of common ground between the Alliance, the Scottish National Party, and the Ecology party on the limited topics we are dealing with. All their manifestos argued for greater investment in housing, the improvement of the housing stock by better grants and other means, and the encouragement of home ownership. The Alliance and the SNP would both have modified the right to buy council houses by allowing local authorities to decide how many to sell, or to apply for the right to impose restrictions. The Ecology party proposed a trust holding scheme which, it was claimed, would give freedom of ownership without depleting the community housing stock. All three parties favoured, expressly or by implication, greater obligations on local authorities to repair and maintain their houses, and all similarly favoured co-operative and neighbourhood enterprise. The SNP would have limited rent increases to 'reasonable' levels, and transferred the debt burden of existing houses to central government, but the Alliance would, in the longer term, have required public authorities to fix rents so that housing accounts balanced, which might have meant very different rent levels. The Ecology party specifically proposed getting empty houses reoccupied and derelict land brought back into use, though this was no doubt implicit in the other two parties' policies. With regard to the pollution of the environment, all three parties embraced the principle that the polluter must pay, and favoured more rigorous legislation and its enforcement. The Alliance and the Ecology party, like the Tories, gave special mention to reducing pollution by encouraging the recycling of used products and materials. In regard to transport, all the three parties favoured public transport, with greater investment in rail and bus services (especially by rail electrification) and the Alliance and the SNP promised road equivalent tariffs for the ferry services, though the Alliance recognised that any problems arising from this must be monitored. As regards roads, all three parties showed signs of trying to face both ways, by recognising that some comprehensive improvements were still necessary, although only the Ecology party proposed to restrict the use of cars, and then in urban areas only.

The Conservative administration will have no need to concede any more to these proposals than they wish to, unless there develops a degree of support for them within the party which seems inconceivable at present. The new government is in a strong position to pursue its manifesto proposals without effective parliamentary opposition unless any of them prove to be impracticable for other reasons than lack of parliamentary support.

What is this likely to mean? There is nothing to prevent the government extending the right to buy council houses and increasing the discount available, giving tenants the right to get repairs done and to be reimbursed by councils (though one hopes that there will be genuine consultations with councils about how this can be fitted in with reasonable programmes for maintenance and repair by councils themselves). Equally the government will be able to make good their promise to put even more emphasis on housing improvement grants and the work of housing associations. What it may find more difficult, in the field of housing, is to ensure that more land is available for private building (since local authorities have their own ideas on what land is suitable and have considerable powers to impose delays) and to get the building societies to play the fuller part proposed for them, because the building societies will refuse to allocate funds in any way which might reduce the confidence of investors. With regard to the rescue of the inner cities, the Tory party (no doubt on the basis of experience as a government) did not commit itself to objectives which may prove beyond the reach of any administration. People are to be encouraged to move back into cities by new housebuilding and by 'homesteading', but no targets were specified; similarly small business schemes and enterprise zones are to encourage business and industry to come back, and efforts are to be increased to bring under-used public sector land back into use. Those cautious promises may prove more capable of being fulfilled than Labour's objective of using 'agreed development plans' at both national and local level to locate investment and jobs in the inner cities, since it remained to be seen, had Labour won the election, whether agreement could be reached on anything effective. On the transport front, the Tory manifesto was noticeably restrained about future spending on road improvements, and the government will have no difficulty in "pressing on" (to quote the manifesto) at what they consider a proper rate. The manifesto was equally restrained on ferry subsidies, emphasising what had been done without referring to the 1979 commitment on road equivalent tariffs. And since the commitment on railways was not a promise but an implied warning - that investment would not go ahead without cost reductions and fewer restrictive practices - there will be no difficulty in a government with a massive majority pursuing that line. On pollution too, the government's commitments (with the exception of the promise to reduce lead pollution and to tighten the controls on hazardous waste) are much less specific and idealistic than many of those in the other party manifestos, and will no doubt be implemented, since they are generalised objectives or not dependent on increased expenditure or the consent of powerful outside interests. No doubt the environmental pressure groups will do their best to secure the maximum possible performance in these fields, but in this as in other respects they, like all those who wish to influence government policy, would do well to recognise that their best prospect of success in the next four or five years must lie in converting the Conservative party, and in particular Conservative MPs, to their point of view.

INDEX